# Death
of a
# Lady's
# Man

# Death
## of a
# Lady's
# Man

Leonard Cohen

ANDRE
DEUTSCH

THIS IS AN ANDRE DEUTSCH BOOK

Text © Leonard Cohen 1978, 2010

This edition published in 2016 by
Andre Deutsch
A division of the
Carlton Publishing Group
20 Mortimer Street
London
W1T 3JW

First published in 1979 by
André Deutsch Limited

A CIP catalogue for this book is available from
the British Library

ISBN: 978 0 233 00300 9

Printed in UK

to Masha Cohen
the memory of my mother

By Leonard Cohen

*Books*
Let Us Compare Mythologies
The Spice-Box of Earth
The Favourite Game
Flowers for Hitler
Beautiful Losers
Parasites of Heaven
Selected Poems, 1956-1968
The Energy of Slaves
Death of a Lady's Man

*Records*
Songs of Leonard Cohen
Songs from a Room
Songs of Love and Hate
Live Songs
New Skin for the Old Ceremony
The Best of Leonard Cohen
Death of a Ladies' Man

# Contents

# I KNELT BESIDE A STREAM

I knelt beside a stream which was manifesting on a polished wooden floor in an apartment above Central Park. A feathered shield was fastened to my left forearm. A feathered helmet was lowered on my head. I was invested with a duty to protect the orphan and the widow. This made me feel so good I climbed on Alexandra's double bed and wept in a general way for the fate of men. Then I followed her into the bathroom. She appeared to turn gold. She stood before me as huge as the guardian of a harbour. How had I ever thought of mastering her? With a hand of chrome and an immense Gauloise cigarette she suggested that I give up and worship her, which I did for ten years. Thus began the obscene silence of my career as a lady's man.

## I KNELT BESIDE A STREAM

*This curious paragraph is obviously distilled from a longer undated journal entry probably written during the spring or summer of 1975. I give it in its entirety.*

Thinking of some times with Alexandra, one night when I wept for the injustice in the world, the promises I made to the weak and fatherless on her double bed. I knelt down beside a stream and I was invested with the high duty to protect them. Someone hooked a feathered shield on my forearm, and lowered a feathered helmet on my head. My left arm armoured, my right arm armoured, the mind fortified. This was not a dream. The stream flowed by me, manifested in a room above the pavement in New York. Later, just before I mastered her, she turned golden in the bathroom, gold and towering, suggesting strongly with an immense chrome hand that I give up and worship her. I think I did. My thighs were so thin she was alarmed. She thought I was starving.

Now I lie in a pool of fat, ashamed before the daisies to be what I am. Eight years ago, and then the obscene silence of my career, while the butchers climbed on the throne, and they hacked the veil away, and they stood there above us grinning, not even bothering to cover themselves. I made a treaty with those who saw, but I broke it under torture. I was divided into three parts. One part was given to a wife, one part was given to money, one part was given to the daisies. And Alexandra herself bound to the world, babies, a cigarette holder, an accent accelerating toward a wordless gargle and swoon in the Poet's Corner. The last time we met, in the lobby of the Algonquin Hotel, I punished her by whispering, "Some of us still take acid."

Distant battles you may say, but God, how ugly your clothes are. You wear them like the ludicrous stripes of bondage. And you are the winners. You are the guards. And even the butchers above you are not in command. I broke under the sentence of loneliness and the wound of my beautiful twin. These veterans are to be avoided, the old campaigns, the view from the foxhole. You can see them tapping away in every garden. And many other spirits complaining, the ground with a voice, the buried fig tree, and now at noon, the sun over the windmill, the signal of the yellow daisies.

## YOUR MOMENT NOW

This is your moment now. I give you the knowledge to distinguish between what is holy and what is common. I touch you with a recollection of your grief. Here you are again, little priest. Bring your heart back to its place.

> Looks like we won't
> be making love at all
>     Too many people watching us
> Looks like we won't
> be meeting at the grill
>     Too many people touching us
> Grease up your ass
> Let's tear our love to pieces
> Your beauty won't be anything
>     when I take off my glasses

Is that what they're singing in the dungeons now? Is that the jingle muttered as slaves touch themselves? It is, O adventurous inspector of the semen'd cells, it is what they're singing.

*But did he bring the "heart back to its place"? We hardly think so. We would say rather that he scattered the heart and made everyone uncomfortable. The piece begins at the centre, somewhat unified and calm, then it claws at its immediate vicinity like Edgar Allan Poe buried alive, then it makes a break for the surface which it achieves at the cost of fragmenting the original physic thrust, and is last seen evaporating among some half-uttered confessions of self-abuse. Reversing the order of the sentences results in a more salutary effect:*

Bring your heart back to its place. Here you are again, little priest. I touch you with a recollection of your grief. I give you the knowledge to distinguish between what is holy and what is common. This is your moment now.

# THE CAFÉ

The beauty of my table.
The cracked marble top.
A brown-haired girl ten tables away.
Come with me.
I want to talk.
I've taken a drug that makes me want to talk.

## THE CAFÉ

*The notebooks indicate that this café was situated near the waterfront in the port of Piraeus. I could not find it. Upon inquiry, I discovered that it had been demolished and the marble tabletops thrown into the harbour. The brunette, who was thin then, is now a skeleton. Her sleeveless summer frock is for sale on Deluth Street on a wire hanger. The little cardboard boxes of Maxiton, the flat sliding metal containers of Rytaline, quite absent from self-service pharmacies. The pretty conversation dissolved immediately into the sunlight which is why it was urgent and breathless. Standing on the quay, I saw some ghostly shapes in the depths but I was told they were sunken Javex bottles.*

# THE CHANGE

I could not trade you for a nightingale. I could not trade you for a hammered golden bird. You took away my music. You set me here with blunted tongue to listen only. Someone is playing a grand piano with two hands. Someone is whispering to her shepherd. I never got to wear my high leather boots. I never became a sign for everything that is high and nervous. You entered me into a quarrel with a woman and you said, This is your voice. You put the moon in a microscope. You dimmed the beauty of everything that is not her and then you dimmed her beauty. I never got to build the barn. Only once did I ride with Kid Marley. Someone is squeezing the old accordion. They are performing the national dance. The patriots have gathered round. O sir, you were so beautiful as a woman. You were so beautiful as a song. You are so ugly as a god.

## THE CHANGE

*I think this qualifies as great religious poetry and also earns itself a place in the annals of complaint. The boots come from Clarence, an aluminum-fronted boutique on the Champs-Elysées. Kid Marley was a rodeo champion from Tennessee who sold the author a lame horse in the late sixties.*

.

# DEATH TO THIS BOOK

    Death to this book or fuck this book and fuck this marriage. Fuck the twenty-six letters of my cowardice. Fuck you for breaking the mirror and throwing the eyebrow tweezers out the window. Your dead bed night after night and nothing warm but baby talk. Fuck marriage and theology and the cold goodnight. Fuck the idolatry of anger and the priests who say so. How dare they. How dare they. Thanks for your judgement on me. Murder and a fast train to Paris and me thin again in my blue raincoat, and Barbara waiting at the Cluny Square Hotel. Fuck her for never turning up.

*The violence of this paragraph is somewhat mitigated by the sense of nostalgia and loss in the last two lines. Does he really wish to negate his life and his work? Although the energy is similar, we get a different picture from the first passage of an unpublished manuscript called My Life in Art, from which many of the pieces of this present volume are excerpted or reworked.*

We begin the Final Revision of My Life in Art. There hasn't been a book like this in a long time. Much of the effort in this ultimate version will be expended trying to dignify a worthless piece of junk. The modern reader will be provided a framework of defeat through which he may view without intimidation a triumph of blazing genius. I have the manuscript beside me now. It took me years to write. During this time you were grinding out your bullshit. It will become clear that I am the stylist of my era and the only honest man in town. I did not quarrel with my voices. I took it down out of the air. This is called work by those who know and should not be confused with an Eastern trance.

## ANOTHER ROOM

I climbed the stairs with my key and my brown leather bag and I entered room eight. I heard Aleece mounting the steps behind me. Room eight. My own room in a warm country. A bed, a table, a chair. Perhaps I could become a poet again. Aleece was making noises in the hall. I could see the ocean in the late afternoon light outside the window. I should look at the ocean but I don't feel like it. The interior voice said, You will only sing again if you give up lechery. Choose. This is a place where you may begin again. But I want her. Let me have her. Throw yourself upon your stiffness and take up your pen.

*She makes a noise in the hallway*
*Come in, I say*
*She comes in*
*Out to the balcony*
*Stand behind her*
*Lean over, I say*
*Up with her skirt*
*Drool in my hand*
*to open it up*
*Watch the sunset*
*over her hair*
*Are you connected*
*to the hotel, the chambermaid perhaps? I say*
*No, I'm the one*
*you are writing about, she says*
*the one who sails down*
*the pillars of blood*
*from brain to isthmus*
*and lost in your unhanded trousers*
*I cause myself to come true*

22

How noble I felt after writing these lines. Aleece had gone away. The emanations of my labour had cleared the hallway. And how much more satisfying this concentration than trifling with a foreign presence or, worse, disturbing another's heart.

## ANOTHER ROOM

*But you <u>have</u> disturbed my heart. Even if my legs are made of stainless steel and a fish circles in the air at the height of my buttocks I am not protected from your agitation of my heart. I am a bee in your world. I am a squirrel. I move too quickly. I die too fast. Your song is cruel and selfish. You have no gasp to express me. I smell so wonderfully sea-like. There is a seaweed bandage, a one-layered seaweed bandage, on something torn in me. It is futile to contact you in the midst of your training but I've been hoping you might fall on a spear and leave your master and live with me on the servicemen's beach behind the Gad Hotel. My legs have been in a jukebox ever since you left. I am Dutch, I am young, I have sailed the world. Bring the fish back to my anus and bring the bee back to your swollen bite. And remember me, Green Eyes, remember your shell-shocked whore and the lather of her ruthless shaving. I appeared in this world with you when you were lost in the pride of being alone. I took you to bath and I took you to bed and I put sand in your mouth by the ocean.*

Forgive me, Aleece, forgive me *is scrawled across the seascape pictured on this giant postcard.*

23

They tell me that Micjel is sick. They say he finally agreed to get de-intoxicated. They will never crush him. His French mind will live forever just behind his throat. He will work all night and every night to see them utterly defeated. He will change folk singing and the love song in particular. The wine is with him and the soil is in his custody. You and I are wanderers.

I often think of you. Many will come to recognize your nobility. I'll shove it down their throats if I have to. We will sell your nobility to every fucking ass-hole who ever dreamed of a better life. That's a promise. It is written.

I have had no fresh fruit for many weeks. And people are wiping juice off their fat lips. Puffed up with their new power and secure in their deceit. They speak for us! They dare! They dare to speak for us! One day this will be over. The war against the poor. Our fury will unfurl. Our fury will uncoil.

Your kisses haunt me and the taste of your kisses and your mouth. I wish for nothing but to see our government established in this hell-hole. Then I'll work on them like I worked on the others. I don't intend to let their freedom choke me. But your tongue is like a Zionist dream that I must put aside.

Nothing is going to happen to everyone. I think we're going to win. The fucking ass-holes are going to get it too. They hate us. I'll live to see them gaping at their lives in utter disbelief. I'll live to see a decent society built around this page.

# OUR GOVERNMENT-IN-EXILE

*This is the work of a middle-class mind flirting with terrorism—not without a certain charm. A modest effort should be made by all concerned to discredit and neutralize this type of inflammatory expression now that the actual business of running the country is in our hands. His thought did have a certain currency among extremists of every persuasion, and he was a familiar figure in the revolutionary cafés of pre-Independence Montreal with his ouija board and Walther PPK automatic. There was inherent, however, in all his positions, an unattractive frivolity which necessarily disqualified him from the responsibilities of leadership. When asked to clarify his stand on certain important matters, he replied, "How can you concern yourself with these things while Layton and I are alive?" After he published the following verses in the influential pages of Le Monde he was deserted by serious men of all shades of opinion.*

I think you are fools to speak French
It is a language which invites the mind
to rebel against itself causing inflamed ideas
grotesque postures and a theoretical approach
to common body functions. It ordains the soul
in a tacky priesthood devoted to the salvation
of a failed erection. It is the language
of cancer as it annexes the spirit and
instals a tumour in every honeycomb
Between the rotten teeth of French are incubated
the pettiest notions of destiny and the shabbiest
versions of glory and the dreariest dogma of change
ever to pollute the simplicity of human action

French is a carnival mirror in which the
brachycephalic idiot is affirmed and encouraged
to compose a manifesto on the destruction of the
   sideshow

I think you are fools to speak English
I know what you are thinking when you speak
   English
You are thinking piggy English thoughts
you sterilized swine of a language that has no
   genitals
You are peepee and kaka and nothing else
and therefore the lovers die in all your songs
You can't fool me you cradle of urine
where Jesus Christ was finally put to sleep
and even the bowels of Satan cannot find
a decent place to stink in your flat rhythms
of ambition and disease
English, I know you, you are frightened by saliva
your adventure is the glass bricks of sociology
you are German with a licence to kill

I hate you but it is not in English
I love you but it is not in French
I speak to the devil but it is not about your
   punishment
I speak to the table but it is not about your plan
I kneel between the legs of the moon
in a vehicle of perfect stuttering
and you dare to interview me on the matter
of your loathsome destinies
you poor boobies of the north
who have set out for heaven with your mouths on fire
Surrender now surrender to each other
your loveliest useless aspects
and live with me in this and other voices

26

like the wind harps you were meant to be
Come and sleep in the mother tongue
and be awakened by a virgin
(O dead-hearted turds of particular speech)
be awakened by a virgin
into a sovereign state of common grace

# THE ABSENCE OF MONICA

She's gone away
   on the morning boat
My heart
   was too young for her
Wind comes over
   the baker's house
sweet with branch
   of burning fir
She'll never comb
   her hair in front of me
I'll never see
   her sweater on a chair
Cinders from the
   chimney float
on the absence
   of Monica
I spent the morning
   with her ghost
We touched the nettles
   painlessly
I carry the bread
   on a piece of string
and now I'm free
   to come and go

# THE ABSENCE OF MONICA

*From the Notebooks:*

Oh the breeze from the baker's oven makes me reel and invent a room with Monica, windows and her sweater over a chair, her rich family and her modesty. I never wanted anything but Monica, to be in a room with her in Europe and to be head of the government-in-exile.

...Excavate the fig tree, elect the municipal council, be kind to the ones in your kitchen, fill up the years without Monica...

She is stretched out on the hill. She came back to me from the middle of the water. She is sailing to Piraeus with a young banker. It is an aspect of her generosity to be in two places at once. Who else is coming to the island? There are only two of you. You and your date in the realms of suffering. How dare you climb on Monica to speak theology? That is why you cannot have the room with her in Rue des Ecoles...

...I buried Monica in this hill, right before my eyes. Some youths violated the site yesterday. They came over the wall when I was inside the house. They got away with a bunch of poppies, actually two poppies, some daisies and a tangle of wild spinach. But they left their ugly footprints here and there. Traces of the unclean boots which have soiled my finest passages...

# DEATH OF A LADY'S MAN

The man she wanted all her life
    was hanging by a thread.
"I never even knew how much
    I wanted you," she said.
His muscles they were numbered
    and his style was obsolete.
"O baby, I have come too late."
    She knelt beside his feet.

"I'll never see a face like yours
    in years of men to come,
I'll never see such arms again
    in wrestling or in love."
And all his virtues burning
    in the smoky holocaust,
she took unto herself
    most everything her lover lost.

Now the master of this landscape
    he was standing at the view
with a sparrow of St. Francis
    that he was preaching to.
She beckoned to the sentry
    of his high religious mood.
She said, "I'll make a space between my legs,
    I'll teach you solitude."

He offered her an orgy
    in a many-mirrored room;
he promised her protection
    for the issue of her womb.

She moved her body hard
    against a sharpened metal spoon,
she stopped the bloody rituals
    of passage to the moon.

She took his much-admired
    oriental frame of mind,
and the heart-of-darkness alibi
    his money hides behind.
She took his blonde madonna
    and his monastery wine.
"This mental space is occupied
    and everything is mine."

He tried to make a final stand
    beside the railway track.
She said, "The art of longing's over
    and it's never coming back."
She took his tavern parliament,
    his cap, his cocky dance;
she mocked his female fashions
    and his working-class moustache.

The last time that I saw him
    he was trying hard to get
a woman's education
    but he's not a woman yet.
And the last time that I saw her
    she was living with a boy
who gives her soul an empty room
    and gives her body joy.

So the great affair is over
    but whoever would have guessed

it would leave us all so vacant
    and so deeply unimpressed.
It's like our visit to the moon
    or to that other star:
I guess you go for nothing
    if you really want to go that far.

Darling, I'm afraid we have to go to the end of love.

*or*

O Darling, I'm afraid that we will have to go to the end of love.

*and many variations, some signed, some unsigned, obviously meant for someone's eyes, written in the margin of this and other pages.*

## MY WIFE AND I

My wife and I made love this afternoon. We hid together from the light of our desire, forehead to forehead. Later she asked me, Did I taste sweet for you? Dear companion, you did. This evening I watched with pleasure as she undressed and put on her flannel pyjamas. I held her closely until she went to sleep. Then I closed the light and left the room carefully and I came down here to you.

## MY WIFE AND I

*Who can go beyond the first four words? Who can hurry past the final six?*

*Poet of the two great intimacies, you have appeared again to unify our grave concerns.*

*Where is she now? Where are these flannel pyjamas? Where is your tenderness to Woman and to God?*

*I know you are cheating somewhere; nevertheless, I consent to be profoundly touched by the exquisite accident of this paragraph.*

*I did not have this work in mind as a child, but I am not ashamed to be your exegete.*

# THE NEWS YOU REALLY HATE

You fucking whore, I thought that you were really interested in music. I thought the heart was somewhat sorrowful. I might have gone with you under the desk and eaten a soft-boiled egg. I'm going to tell my baby brother not to do what I have done. I'm going to tune you until the string breaks. The Communists do not know how evil you really are.

We are different from you. That's the news you really hate. That's the news to ring the bells and start the fires while your boyfriend serves you the hair-ball lunch. I have been admitted through the stained-glass shadows where your stench is unwelcome. How dare you pay us any attention? I'm going to eat now. I have declared war on you forever and ever. Disguised as a hat I will rip off your eyebrows. I am going to be here in the sun for a long time. The fragrance comes up again. It does not reach you. It does not invite you to close your eyes in the storm. The trumpets cry up inside me and my king is home. I am judged again with mercy.

*If we affirm human life, and do not habitually surrender ourselves to the many-sided argument, it is sometimes refreshing to embrace a position of uncompromising unforgiveness. As the poet shows, there are surprises and rewards that follow in the wake of the undiluted expression of one's hateful seizures.*

*However, if you are unskilled in the subtle transformative processes of language, it is best not to write down your ugly thoughts. If you must, do not show them to one who has the power to transmute. He will not be able to help you. He cannot recover from what he himself has begun.*

# I HAVE TAKEN YOU

I have taken you
I have fucked you
I have made love to you
In rooms and courtyards
    we have given ourselves to passion
Swords of angels
    crossed over our nakedness
to make love secret in the world
Nothing was withheld
All was generosity and true appetite
Why is it
    even when you smile saying
yes now whenever
    whenever you want me
why is it I do not believe
    I will ever hold you again
or walk on the street
    under my hood
with your sweet juices dried fragrant
    on my lips and fingers
It makes me want to renounce you
and discover flaws in your buttocks
and cinders in the light of your face
I wait for you to damage my appetite
so I can be something more
    than a hungry man
waiting for the feast
with someone less hungry than he is

## I HAVE TAKEN YOU

*In lines 15 and 16 he asks a question which he does not answer. Beyond a general sense of his dis-ease, he never makes clear the actual mechanics of his anxiety. If "Nothing was withheld/ All was generosity...," why should he "not believe/ I will ever hold you again..."? This poem fails because something has been "withheld" from the reader. There is a lie here, or a deep stinginess with the truth. The poem begins to rot after the third line, maybe after the second. We cannot believe in his "we," and we cannot believe in his "our." What happened between them escapes this poem. Their mutuality requires the most obvious crutches of Victorian syntax just to limp down the page. He never knew who she was. She never revealed herself to him. He never even asked her the question. It is his hunger only that is the source of his anxiety. It is the solitude of his hunger that terrifies him into a monkish consideration of giving up her ass. Her ass is still upstairs, and he's up there with it. The poem should read:*

> I fucked you
> now I want to find
> the flaw in your buttocks
> the cinder
> in the light of your face

## IT WOULD BE CRUEL

It would be cruel to tell you that you are not prettier than your sister anymore, so I won't tell you. I won't even write it down. But I will remember it every time you ask me for something which only beauty can demand. Friends that are dead or broken, your face and your body can't shelter them now. Many people are beyond my protection. They always were. But I had such strength when you were beautiful. Earlier this evening I thought, At least tonight I have not added to my bitterness.

# IT WOULD BE CRUEL

*At the very end of the first book of the Final Revision of My Life in Art we find:*

That is the end of the story except to tell you how she became beautiful. As if I knew. The wind keeps slamming the shutter and then throwing it open to expose to the lane the lurid sight of one at his table. Twice I've had to chase a thin dog away from the garbage. It is a fierce night. There is no question that moon will survive the clouds. As surely as the brain can clear she has become beautiful.

*However, toward the end of the third book of the Final Revision of My Life in Art he has another fit:*

I don't want you to lie down. You can't open your legs in here. Yes, sometimes I think you are pretty. This is almost one of the times. It does make a difference. You have overpriced yourself. You would have to be blonde for that. You would have to break my heart just combing your hair. You don't. I don't forgive you anymore on account of your round buttocks. The hustle is over. Only my victories restrain you.

*But she did become very beautiful. She was photographed lying down by two hundred naked men. Egyptian women fell out of the fume to lie beside her and stain her fingernails. Their cats tried to fall down too, but she would not let them leave the air.*

# I DECIDED

I decided to jump literature ahead a few years. Because you are angry, I decided to infuriate you. I am infected with the delirious poison of contempt when I rub my huge nose into your lives and your works. I learned contempt from you. Philistine implies a vigour which you do not have. This paragraph cannot be seized by an iron fist. It is understood immediately. It recoils from your love. It has enjoyed your company. My work is alive.

# I DECIDED

*Did he "jump literature ahead a few years"?*
*Certainly, this phase of his work constitutes one of the*
*fiercest attacks ever launched against both the*
*"psychological" and "irrationalist" modes of expression.*
*There is a new freedom here which invites, at the very*
*least, a new scheme of determinism. There is also a*
*willing sense of responsibility and manliness such as we*
*do not find among the current and endless repetitions of*
*stale dada-ist re-discovery. There are guidelines here that*
*will take us well into the two-thousands. He has indicated*
*a process, perhaps even sketched out the handbook, by*
*which we may go to "the end of love." I love this boy, not*
*yet out of his middle-age. He taught me how to breathe*
*and he gave me a dungeon to roast my heart in and a*
*view of the noble cartoon. But listen to him now, in the*
*Notebooks, as he approaches his own doubt in the matter:*

So it ends, my conversation with the song. Not so
sweetly as it began, but still pleasantly unimportant. I
almost tried to make a living with it. Deep down the
genius plots his crooked revenge. Change all taste
around and make this page an anthem of the change.
I'd rather listen to something else... Consign this all
to eccentricity. Affirm the mainstream, everyone.

## THE BEETLE

Do not be frightened. Where is the beetle I gave you? It is a companion for you somewhere in the room. Here is my peace. These tears will help you. I placed you at a table in the middle of the night. I let you move toward your pain. I let you come near. I let you come in. Now you have no names for yourself. Now you are my creature. This is the mercy. These are the clean tears. You may speak to me now. I will not take your work from you. Have you tired of my mercy? Have you wept enough? Have you seized an image of me? This is the voice of one turning aside. This is my holy work. It has changed the world since you began this word and you are still reading the instructions. Where is your beetle? It pleased you not to want to murder it. An oath of friendship between you and your beetle came to your lips. It was touching. You pleased yourself with your mercy. Stay with me. You are the beetle I do not crush, so busy in the light of my eyes. This is the room I prepared for you. It is here you will prepare the marriage. You will untarnish it. You will sweep the chamber where I form my worlds. Now you may have back your stone heart. Someone walks by your window, a slight limp in his step. You cannot see outside and this is my world also. Come to me again when you are not tired, when your panic makes you alert to me, and the perfection of my world bends you down in shame.

## THE BEETLE

*Is there a modern reader that can measure up to this page? Is there one quiet enough? Is there one who has prepared herself? Is there a wall in Los Angeles on which such a beetle could appear?*

*I have been sitting still for two hours in a cabin on a mountain. The crickets give a pulse to the night. A fly bangs around inside my lampshade. His book lies open before me but I do not know how to approach the purity of this passage.*

*In all the scriptures of the West, has God ever spoken so gently?*

## ORION

Orion is above the house. I am sealed into the lower room for some hours of the night. I am trying to cheat you. I am trying to go ahead without you. Slavic music, a Greek cigarette, the beautiful light of two oil lamps, just like the good old days. Turn off the radio. Sit and wait for me. Wait for my voice. You could have spoken of my beauty when I came to you in the form of a woman a few moments ago but you had no hospitality for me, engrossed as you were in a scheme. Now you don't have the scheme and you don't have the energy of my image. Even your idolatry is paralysed.

## *ORION*

Orion is above the house

*He works under the sign of the Hunter. A clumsy effort to mythologize his appetite. His greed is enormous. He even tries to appropriate the constellation. As if he has secured it by a kite string.*

I am sealed...

*He is not locked, he is sealed, that is, affirmed, guaranteed and authenticated by the very nature of the enterprise.*

I am trying to cheat you

*He invokes The Other with a confession of impotence, exile and separation.*

46

Turn off the radio
*The first command. The Other begins to manifest.*

Sit and wait for me
*The Other proposes, but we are as yet unaware of the exact aspect of the suggested intimacy.*

... the form of a woman ...
*Western doctors have determined that the form of a woman appears to a middle-aged man something like once every fifteen seconds. He could have ended his suffering by embracing her but four times a minute he refused his salvation.*

... engrossed as you were in a scheme ...
*The mutiny of the conceptual mind, clinging to a plot, chained to the Hunt, tyrannized by a static vision of Heaven, Lucifer's addiction to light and his subsequent fall from grace so he might define himself forever in relation to the darkness....*

Now you don't have the scheme and you don't have ... my image
*The Other has dissolved into the pure information of a compassionate rebuke.*

Even your idolatry is paralysed.
*The prelude to surrender. His view of the exile has been irreparably damaged. He knows why he is in hell.*

*Two years later, in the Notebooks, we find:*

Let the explanation be
the Hunter poised above me
flowing through his useless forms
of predatory majesty

47

## TO DEAL WITH YOU

And now to deal with you. I am glad that you no longer consider yourself "God's exclusive pet." I sincerely hope that we do not have to be privy to any more of your voices. You are not Joan of Arc. It was a crude charlatan's trick, trying to associate the obscurity of your style with the mystery of the godhead. This and nothing else is my voice. It is in you. It has caught into you and it is there like sexual desire.

## TO DEAL WITH YOU

A man has set a fishhook in his lip. Does this mean we can believe what he says? Does he think of himself as the catch or the bait? Is anyone bored enough to reel him in? This paragraph is, I believe, an invitation for the truly bored to come out of the closet and be baffled one more time, one last time. Those who do not rest forever in a vindicated hostility, those who can read past the vindication, will discover deep in the strata of their boredom the fuel of a great activity. The mouth of the napping critic will be torn away. The disfiguring yawn of brotherhood will be penetrated. They will begin to talk to themselves.

# THE ALTAR

There is a certain power in this book that cannot be denied even though you try to deny it in every word. Deny it here. Am I less disgusting than you are? Am I happier? Near the beginning of the Bible I am told how to build the Altar. It is to be raised with unhewn stones. You are such a sad hewer of stones. And you are an amusing enemy, especially when you discover for us all your standards of hewn stone. You may worship here. You can rip a heart out on this paragraph.

## THE ALTAR

*There are many hearts baking on this altar. There is the heart behind the beautiful brown nipple that would not erect itself. There is the heart of one who tried to follow in my footsteps when I had stopped moving. There is the heart of one high above me who stooped to become my rival. There is the heart of the idolator who said that God was Love alone. My maid's heart is there, who served me too long. There is the heart that did not believe in the stone knife. There is the heart that envied and the heart that surrendered to the anonymity of this miracle. Among these few that I have offered there is my own, the heart of a translator who has tried to render into common usage the high commands of pure energy, who has not denied his own inclination to obey. If these hearts of mine are badly carved it is because THE ALTAR seduced me into a mood of happy careless butchery.*

# THE HOUSE

I have been commanded to make a house for your restless thoughts so you can sleep beside your wife in peace. This is the house for your anger, your envy, your sloth, your judgements, all your restless thoughts. I am not speaking to myself. You are familiar with this house. It is not here that we reason together. This is the house you must leave to be free. Children, this house cannot be seen. You have already experienced it although I do not depend on your honesty. I would rather listen to Hitler's table talk than build this house, let alone live in it. The wife in your arms will die. The child on your knees will be cut down. You cannot cross this out. There is no ceremony in this house. There is no woman being born. I cannot dignify your vigil by the window. Songs from the parchment infect my ear. We huff and we puff and we blow the house down.

## THE HOUSE

*This fails. THE HOUSE is still there. A breath from the nursery cannot bring it down. He built it too strong. It becomes the fortress of the enemy where he himself is held prisoner. Nor will this book dissolve into ordinary conversation. It is too weak to embrace the world. We are in the hands of an eccentric, but his eccentricity is significant insofar as we can infer from it a regular orbit of existence which, unfortunately, has evaporated. How ironic that the little evidence we have of the former sanity is in the achievement of this idiot.*

## THIS MARRIAGE

I said, Because it is so horrible between us I will go and stop Egypt's bullet. Trumpets and a curtain of razor blades. Organ music. She said, That's beautiful. Then I can commit suicide and the child falls into strangers' hands. The radio said, He helped a lot of people, but the good they do die young, I just looked around and he was gone. I said. She said. The monstrosities of Lilith attack her. Yug, yug, yug, she said. What you did to me, I said. The lonely, we said. The nights of hands on ourselves. Your unkindness, we said. Your greed. Your unkindness. Your bitter tongue. Give me time. You never learn. Your ancestors. My ancestors. Fuck you, I said. You shit. Stop screaming. I can't stand it. You can't stand anything. Nobody can live like this. In front of the child. Let him learn. This is no good. Yer fuckn right it's no good. This kitchen was once beautiful. Oil lamps, order, the set table. Sabbath observed. That's what I want. You don't want it. You don't know what I want. You don't know anything about me. You never did. Not in the beginning. Not now.

In the realms where this marriage was sealed, where the wedding feast goes on and on, where Adam and Eve face one another, the foundations are faultless and secure, your beast's hair flares like black fire upward and your breasts, now in maidenhood, now in motherhood, draw down my face, our hunger blessed by sun and moon, a ring of dancers round the house where within the room is hid, where within the bed is undone, whereupon the hunger's joined, where within the one speaks himself expressions yet unknown.

## THIS MARRIAGE

*THIS MARRIAGE is locked. It is difficult to enter. It is a marriage and operates like one, healing itself the moment it is condemned. In every house there is this marriage which cannot be explained. In our day it appears fragile and easily violated, but it is still the profoundest initiation, and one into which no stranger can intrude.*

## THIS MARRIAGE

*Long before morning I came to this page. It does not seem to admit me. It is like marriage itself. In every house on the street there is a marriage which cannot be explained. This is the profoundest initiation into which no stranger can intrude. This is the cemetery of love, where love is most forgiven and most adored.*

## THIS MARRIAGE

*He hangs a crown over his filthy kitchen and expects us to put our hands together and say Grace.*

# THE PHOTOGRAPH

My dark companion photographs me among the daisies.
My life in art.
She is beautiful when she smiles.
She should smile more often.
We have the same nature.
We are lazy and fascinating.
One day we will go back to that creek in Tennessee
and she will shoot me with a .22.
Take one with my hat on.
We have lots of film.
I taught her how to greet a man in the morning.
These things have been lost
like the arch and the goldenrods.
She asked me to teach them to her—
forgotten modes I happen to remember.
I told her about the time
Adam and Eve tried to commit suicide
but unformed infants of the Milky Way
raised a house against them.
Some of the daisies are up to my thigh.
It is very bright.
The daisies shine back at the sun.
The wind polishes the air.
Some fool might try to pick out a lamentation.
Take one of us together.

## THE PHOTOGRAPH

I taught her...
I told her...

*The stink of pride rises from this garden.*
*Examine this suppressed passage from the original*
*manuscript of My Life in Art:*

> You are to create an angel. Not an Angel of the High,
> obviously not one of the Host. An earthly Angel, the
> Shadow of an Angel. It is to be a collection of energies,
> a ganglion of light and loving-kindness. It will be
> invisible but it will exist in this world. It will move
> through the world in the service of ——. You must
> refine this message. It is still unclear to you. This is the
> nature of your work in the garden. When the Angel
> removes its beggar's clothes it will be invisible and it
> will nourish everything.

## IT'S PROBABLY SPRING

So-and-so is sick of all the shit but doesn't feel that bad today because it's probably Spring. The laundry in the sunshine tells the obscene family story of power and love but it doesn't matter because it's probably Spring. Jack is fat and Jane is twisted from the Plague but you don't have to choose today because it's probably Spring. You're nothing like the pilot, nothing like the matador, you're nothing like the one I waited for, but I won't rub your nose into everything you haven't done because it's probably Spring. I can listen to the bugle now, I can stand beside the old windmill, I can think about my loyal dog buried in the snow. Sally lost her fragrance and her broken heart won't show but she's going to bite her lip and start again because it's finally Spring. The little lambs are leaping through the Easter hoop so the insomniac can get to sleep but he's caught without his knife and fork because it's probably Spring. It's probably Spring. You can give away your money for an hour. You can resume your childhood plan. You're naked and the snake is hungry but the vicious thing won't sting because it's probably Spring. All the poison clouds have settled in a thimble which you nearly make me drink but then you smash it in the fireplace because it's probably Spring. But let's be quiet so we can hear the naval band. They're fine-looking lads and they're playing the National Hymn. Their sweat is sweet beneath the woollen uniforms, it's hot and scratchy but they'll be in white tomorrow because of it's being probably Spring. It is the passion of our Lord. It is the ladder through her hair. It is a lovely field which you cannot find in the city. It is what you can never find again so tender and so wild, so do kneel down and honour what the Name makes manifest because it's probably Spring. O stand in due respect for that which flings your wife into another's arms, which heaves the poppy shrapnel through your heart, which invites you to forgive some shabby crime you're likely to commit because it's probably Spring.

## IT'S PROBABLY SPRING

*I would like to lose my faith in this poet, but I can't. I would like to say that I have discovered in him something glib. I want to disqualify him. He comes too close to betraying me. He comes too close to reeling me in. I want to say that he was too rich. I want to prove that his marriage was happy. I want to say that I only thought he was that good because I misunderstood him. But I am afraid I do not misunderstand him. I understand him. Tonight I understand him perfectly as I sit here heavy with Chinese food under the royal-blue sky of the Los Angeles night, with very little going for me (as they say down here), with much gone sour, but never mind, I do not know how to begin to earn your attention. There is a mood for which Beethoven is too loud, and Bach too wise, and silence too good for a filthy heart such as beats in my breast, but I take my comfort from the creaky hurdy-gurdy tune cranked out uselessly by the one I follow morning and night on a whim of love and a gambler's chance. Tears are close but the Kleenex is too near to make this a great occasion. I read the piece again and again, so pleased that the poet has taken such pains not to touch me. If only I had touched her this lightly, I might not be sitting here now.*

## ANOTHER FAMILY

Sister in the snow, I took another family
and you did not, I took two children out of my knee.
Your brother has fallen down to be cold again —
on his palm he offers two small figures to the white
                                                    storm

I couldn't get away, I took another childhood,
I broke my promise not to go back, and it's cold.
I broke my promise not to suffer, and now
I have to start all over again to earn my solitude

Your mistake is elegant, mine is clumsy,
my scarf is wet and I can't think about myself.
Please be proud of your crystal, your well-made crystal
which does not leak and where you don't shiver

You can be no one and I must be my father,
haunting another childhood with my panic,
and I was meant to be frozen beside you, frozen
                                                    upright
above the goldfish in the solid silver waterfall

and I have to forget what I hate, I have already
begun to forget, it is not hatred anymore, it is
the old childhood, my father's heart attack,
and long instructions about my buttons and my shoes

I left my lover to sit at the head of the table.
My wife has to wonder where I've been
and I have to explain that she was wrong, I was
never strong, I was merely frozen with my sunlight in
                                                    the ice

Now you are alone, you are truly alone,
you were the one who remained standing,
and I betrayed the ending, I fell down under the big
                                                    snowflakes
just like my father, just like his father

and I don't care about anyone again, they can all
go to hell, it is the only luxury down here
where everything changes into nothing new, and you
wait to be cut down in revenge by your duplicate




## ANOTHER FAMILY

*What unfreezes a man? By whose authority
does he admit the Gulf Stream into his crystal? How does
the humiliated spirit find its way out of the dead Kabala?
How to smear the ideal with possibility and then humble
every possibility? Why is nothing left standing? What
removes the skill from his caress and leaves his hand
amputated from all meaning, lifeless and heavy on her
thigh? Why is he born again without a monument?
Either you know why you have come into this world or
you don't.*

# I SHOULD NOT SAY YOU

I should not say you. I should say O. Now I see why they said, the Name. I crumble before the Name. My heart is stubborn before the Name. Give my heart ease in the presence of the Name. My heart is like something that waits. My heart longs to be a chamber for the Name. I am ignorant. I don't know how to make a place for the Name. I lose the Name in my thrust of greed. I lose it in my mind. This heart is dead. This heart hoards its death. It will not make a place for the Name. Fill me with the Name O most high. I swim in your love but I drown in loneliness. End my waiting. Allow me the Name. Protect me in the terror of your absent Name.

Not by oracles. Not by the Bible. Not by ghosts. Not by spirits seen in a magic lens. Not in shadows. Not in braided manes. Not by appearance in the air. Not by the stars at birth. Not by meteors. Not by winds. Not by sacrificial appearances. Not by the entrails of animals sacrificed. Not by the entrails of a human sacrifice. Not by the entrails of fishes. Not by sacrificial fire. Not by red-hot iron. Not by clamp. Not by muzzle. Not by smoke from the altar. Not by the counting of petals. Not by the signal of wings. Not by mice. Not by birds. Not by a cock picking up grains. Not by the layers of the mountain. Not by the strength of the moon. Not by herbs. Not by water. Not by fountains. Not by a wand. Not by dough of cakes. Not by the falling of sticks. Not by meal. Not by salt. Not by dice. Not by ladders. Not by the flight of an arrow. Not by a balanced hatchet. Not by a suspended ring. Not by a stone on a thread. Not by pebbles drawn from a heap. Not by mirrors. Not by writings in ashes. Not by a change of kings. Not by dreams. Not by the lines of the hands. Not by nails reflecting the sun's rays. Not by numbers. Not by drawing lots. Not by passages in books. Not by the letters forming the name of a person. Not by features. Not by the mode of laughing. Not by the pattern of snakes. Not by walking in a circle. Not by drawing a circle. Not by the rings on the finger. Not by dropping melted wax in water. Not by clouds. Not by currents.

Without the Name the wind is a babble, the flowers are a jargon of longing. Without the Name I am a funeral in the garden. Waiting for the next girl. Waiting for the next prize. Without the Name sealed in my heart I am ashamed. It is not sealed. I am ashamed. Without the Name I bear false witness to the glory. Then I am this false witness. Then let me continue.

# THE ASTHMATIC

Because you will not overthrow your life. You cannot breathe. Because of the panic of homelessness. You cannot breathe. Because you have begun to worship time. You cannot breathe. Because you will never have the beautiful one. You cannot breathe. Because you will not sail into the small harbour and enter the village. You cannot breathe. Because your sorrow will not return to its birthplace. You cannot breathe. Because you believe you were not meant to be so far away. You cannot breathe. Because this is the valley of the shadow of death. You cannot breathe. The boat has brought you here. The butterfly sealed your escape. Because you cannot be here. You cannot breathe. The butterfly smashed into a silver tray and sealed your escape like a stone rolled into a tunnel. You cannot breathe. Because you do not know what is coming. You cannot breathe. Because this world is yours and it is not yours. You cannot breathe. Because you rest, because you strive, because you do not work. You cannot breathe. Because you let the world come between you and me. You cannot breathe. Because of an idea of the calm breath. You cannot breathe. Here they have orange and lemon trees. Here there are baths of mineral waters. Because you want to choose a way. You cannot breathe. Because you find the language to welcome me. You cannot breathe. The sun is sparkling all over the blue water. The stony shore is laved by the sea. Yellow curtains are sucked against the portholes. The propeller wants everyone to go to sleep. You separate yourself from an unknown woman in a green sweater. Because of your love of conquering. You cannot breathe. Because you will not address me as an

64

equal. Because you have commanded the guards to shut down the doors and take away breathing. Because the world is stamped with order, like a seal in formless wax. Because you have a God of justice. Because the justice is immediate and flawless. You cannot breathe. Because you cannot uphold your separation. Because your strangerhood is defeated. Because you breathe your breath through the mask of purity. Because you consign to the pale of objectivity her green sweater, the flashing islands, your distance from love, and your whole breathless predicament. You cannot breathe.


## THE ASTHMATIC

*Exposure to this page can induce a suffocating attack in those who are prone to express the condition of profound indecision which asthma probably is. These sinister rhythms betray the quack and we behold the subversive and imperial intention of a mind that wishes to enslave existence in the name of sweet salvation. Here is the old weapon disguised as charity; greed disguised as the usual prayer, and his trap of panic as an invitation to self-reform. I have begun to turn against this man and against this book.*

# THE LOVER AFTER ALL

You die exactly in that attitude of scorn, you filthy parasite of the worthless ordeal. You die looking exactly like that, in all constipated possession of your high degree. You scum on the sunlight, agent of rot in my great sea-faring heart. It is you. It is your wretched judgement of my love affair.

A white butterfly flickers like the end of a home movie, and it gives me words, and with them I can make a world for you to hustle in, a large world, complex and true, where I turn out to be the lover after all, and you turn out to be merely stupid, but forgiven in a hail of seeds.

How can I put you to sleep? What carved stone, what inscription, would keep you down? You hate me because I have no temple. On your fatigue we raise the sign of victory. We inhale deeply the fragrance of your surrender. It is exactly noon. I am the false voice of the armistice. Who waits behind your idiot eyes for the final blow?

## THE LOVER AFTER ALL

*Even though you outwit me, I'm not going back to you. Even though the purity of your love is affirmed by the unanimous quiver of every feather in the celestial host, I am not going back to the axe of your love, O triumphant husbandman and lassoo king of the gateless horses, I am not going back to you, even though I squirm in your arms and surrender to your will the total essence of my dusty shell here in this captured sweat-hall, I am never coming back, I swear by the rent curtain of my virginity and the blood-thick silence between the bridgeless worlds, that I will lie to you forever, and I will be never again the cup of your need.*

I can't stand the sound of slate being scraped. That's what you are doing in my middle ear. This is how they make a spy confess. I came here to find out why you are ugly. The noon bells govern a side of the sky. They are finally tiling that roof up the hill. You are at the centre of your world. We are trying to circumcise your heart. But you cannot stop me from screaming. Yes, we have muffled your voice. You must, you must, you must. This leaves us with a sense of the morning.

## A SENSE OF THE MORNING

*You've had your say. Your fractured morning.*
*Your sentences of oil and water. We don't want to stay*
*with you anymore. Nobody does. You cannot marry ants*
*and raindrops. People have a right to avoid your farm.*
*These misshapen harnesses and aimless straps — who are*
*they for and what labour will you press them into? —*
*deformed spirits meant to die that you revive with thirsts*
*of curiosity and revenge. Someone else has declared war*
*on you. We find it in the Notebooks:*

Do not persecute me for not being beautiful
and do not pretend that I am a little girl
who has not yet learned to use make-up
Do you really want to fight me to the death?
I have children I must live for
You have only Beauty

# KEFI

Last night I made love to the creature, great strength in my hips. I do not have an opinion on the matter. I agree with your opinions. When the wind blows and the daisies swivel, I am in the midst of a glory. I have great kefi this morning, caused by breakfast and strenuous meditation. There is a flag behind the almond blossoms. A passing garbage man on a grey mule yells at me: "I forgive you. Your boasting is like the flower in my teeth. Nevertheless, gringo, you should learn that my way is better."

## KEFI

*These imaginary conversations with sages of the third world! At last Edgar Guest has found his way into the dark corners of colonialism.*

# YOUR GIRL

Put her somewhere
    leaning against a wall
naked on your bed
    dressed up for the ball
Put some thoughts
    in her head
Put some money
    in her hand
Be sure that you can make her come
at least a second time
Brother, that's your girl

*YOUR GIRL*

and speak together of the coming age
when you will put on woman's flesh
and let your beauty once again engage
the courage of a heart to start afresh

do inform my loneliness with moments
of the coming unity, do confess
your body to my utter ignorance
and rest the dreamer from his dreamlessness

*:mysterious quatrains from the Notebooks in which he
tries to sue for peace*

## I BURY MY GIRL FRIEND

You ask me how I write. This is how I write. I get rid of the lizard. I eschew the philosopher's stone. I bury my girl friend. I remove my personality from the line so that I am permitted to use the first person as often as I wish without offending my appetite for modesty. Then I resign. I do errands for my mother, or someone like her. I eat too much. I blame those closest to me for ruining my talent. Then you come to me. The joyous news is mine.

# I BURY MY GIRL FRIEND

*In a recent Notebook we find, perhaps, a more accurate version of the process:*

I pray that no one believes
that your furnaces burn in my ears
and my ears dance away with your skull
that I am yours & you are mine for all
time. I pray that no one believes
that I walk through the night on your breath
and you focus the limbs on my bed
and you ride me on rays of the sun
through the fingerprint forms of your world
I pray that no one can tell
that I am the stone in his shoe
that I fish in a woman's womb
for the pattern of snowflakes to come

# THE PROMISE

A wound in the shoulder keeps me still. The lizards sing, the sea pours in, the night upholds my promise.

I am guarded against your scorn by a spider on the ceiling and a lizard on the wall.

Adam and Eve hang from a thorn, back to back. I want them to face each other.

I will call her out of the used-up sea. I will speak her down from the pitch of terror. She will form her body around the words of longing. She will establish her beauty on the Promise of Faithfulness.

I make this promise now. The other men say: Can you?

Do you wish to see her radiant? "She will establish her beauty on the Promise of Faithfulness." Do you wish to see her radiant? "No, I want to see her cunt." This ambiguity is honoured so you can bear the company.

In one form only does she recognize me, the form of wife. In every other form she is searching for her mate; she blunders past me like something going blind, a salmon or a sea turtle, and I am landscape and water, going the other way.

# THE PROMISE

Crickets and lizards make lace out of the edges of my thought. They're taking me away from the Guerrero. For crimes I did against the heart.
I never thought I'd see a moth and a lizard fighting. The moth is now some darkness in the green translucent belly. No it isn't worth it. It isn't worth it at all. They've launched two red ants against the throne.
I eat too much when I'm with her. I become obscure.
Thank you for killing the moth. I never liked them.
What was the Mexican girl singing to my daughter? My wife was speaking. We were in another room. The wishbone of the song came through. The baby no more crying. The pelican with pierced breast. I was your bride all afternoon and you with the other woman. The other woman carried her here but I am your baby's mother. Cling to her or cling to me, it never makes a difference. You'll open a door in your promise and leave us both alone.

*from the Notebooks 1973*

# THE OTHER VILLAGE

Sometimes I take a moment off and I remember the village and the people I used to know. I remember how we read each other's thoughts. Then I say to myself: What is the use of remembering. I long for them and the sweet taste of their company. No longing can raise the stones on each other again or pull back the sea from the orchards. I live near a different part of the sea. The hawks present their wings to the sky straight and muscled. Close by, my baby daughter, crying, sounds like the child of another people.

## THE OTHER VILLAGE

*When it comes to lamentations*
*I prefer Aretha Franklin*
*to, let's say, Leonard Cohen*
*Needless to add, he hears a different drum*

# THE OLD DAYS

A most beautiful woman chose me. I lived in her palace. She douched all the time. Her hair was naturally perfect. She needed only water, a comb and the sun. I thought the world must be like this. Goodbye darling my destiny is to wander from one palace to another.

> The slums of love
> the slums of love
> now I live in the slums of love
> the crumbs of love
> the crumbs of love
> now I live on the crumbs of love

I am a humble lover living on the crumbs of love. There isn't much to my house not much more than a shack really. Come in you juicy thing I'll let you touch the crumbs of love.

> the crumbs of love
> the crumbs of love
> I'll let you touch the crumbs of love

This is an unaccustomed pleasure. We rarely have a song in this neighbourhood. Bit of sunlight, isn't it? Just like the old days. I'll have to tell the missus when she gets back from the beauty parlour. I'll have to tell her I was visited by one like you.

## THE OLD DAYS

*Tell no one*
*how I visit you*

# A WORKING MAN

I had a wife and children
I got drunk on Saturday night
I went to work every day
I hated the rich
I wanted to fuck a college girl
I was proud to be a working man
I hated the assholes
     who run the revolution
The ones like me will win
We do not need words
You are all on your knees
     looking for the lost nipple
We stand here
We are already above you
Soon the law will be ours
Soon you will experience our mercy
I have no friends
I have no class
There is no we
I had to play on your social illusions
     to get you here in the middle of the night
Dip your flags in the blood
Light your torches
The women are waiting
     in buttoned white dresses
Your dignity is restored

## A WORKING MAN

*We don't give a shit about all this so don't try to threaten us with hints of a New Order. The beings that hover round this table have already overthrown the World and shoved it back up your asshole exactly the same as it was before.*

# APPROACHING THE THRONE

Let's ask the soldier for a song. His cupped match lights up a youthful face. He'll be dead soon. He turns toward us the broad back of his greatcoat. He won't sing Lili Marlene. Why did you kill the highway, the moods of the traveller? This is your mind when you have abandoned me. My priest has not been born. My people have not been born. My wife is sleeping. I have not built the angels around her. O my enemy, how long will you go on judging me from your little pile of shit? End my disgrace in your temple. Look what I have to smite you: Bibles and jawbone and razor straps, but most of all an intimacy with your heart as you sit there wondering whether it is right or wrong, this cry from my throat that has broken down the defenceless world forever.

# THE UNCLEAN START

I went down to the port with my wife. On the way down I accused her of continuing her relentless automatic assault on the centre of my being. I knew this was not wise. I only meant to rap her on the knuckles and direct her attention to her habitual drift toward bitchiness but I lost control. There is no control in these realms. I became a thug. I attacked her spirit. Her spirit armed itself and retaliated massively. I think we were talking about valises or which of us travelled the lightest. A truce was investigated briefly by shabby deputies neither of which had the authority to begin the initiative. You always carry something extra, a shopping bag, something of string and paper that can't be checked. I'm glad you didn't pack for me. You always slow me down. I can't be an acrobat when you're around. You're sandpaper. I can't be a dancer. I'm dead when you're around. You kill. It is your nature. Observe your nature. The shoemaker looked up at us as we passed his open doorway. This humiliation made me furious. I shoved a razor blade into her nerves. Her eyes changed colour. This was done by saying Jesus Christ, quickening my step slightly, minutely moving my jaw, rejecting the essence of her totally and forever. If she went down quickly I would nurse her back to love in time to get her blessings before the boat came in. But why should I, she didn't rub my back when I threw my shoulder out, even when I asked her three times. And why should she since I had defeated her smile over and over. And why should I since she was the enemy of my freedom and the smiling moon over my gradual death. And why should she since I hated her because her beauty died. Why should I because there must be a woman in Jerusalem or beside me on the airplane. Half asleep Old John saw us but it was no humiliation since he didn't recognize me anymore and I no longer greeted him. Captain Mad Body saw us but it didn't matter because he was mute and crazy and lived on the port and knew the shames of everyone. We were on the port, in plain sunlight between the masts and the shops. The shit piled up in the One Heart which is the engine of our energy. We are married: there is only one heart. On common ground the armoured spirits tried to embrace but they both fell down paralysed. Pain removed the world. They felt for the organs of sex but they were gone. There was no war, no peace, no world, the punishment of marriage spoiled. There is no Armageddon here. And fuck you. And fuck you. The horn, the boat was coming. I would have to travel without her blessing in the collapsed world. I won't accuse you of ruining my trip. I won't accuse you of ruining your absence. The *Kamelia* came in, its white decks above us, or was it the *Portokalios Ilios*. I know the name of a boat or two. I always hide her beauty from myself until it is too late to praise her for it. Ropes were flying, uniforms flashing, everywhere haste advised and the threat of lost time. I stared at her as she became beautiful and calm. I would not get the blessing. The journey had an unclean start. And she must carry still-born blessings up the hill.

## THE UNCLEAN START

*In the Final Revision of My Life in Art this passage expands as follows:*

What a burden for the woman being born to carry still-born blessings up the hill. When she got home she pinned a blue ribbon to the inside of my windbreaker, next to where the heart would be. She showed me this much later. Certainly a factor in my coming back alive. I must study the hatred I have for her, how it is transmuted into desire by solitude and distance

*(and where is the hatred now, years later, as he types this out, his love for her aching through the slow-motion snowstorm of her absence)*

Without her blessing I didn't have the courage or joy to greet the sea or the milky shores of islands or the mountain villages of faded silver. I had these in mind from happier sitings but I couldn't call them out. I felt unworthy of the landscape, present and past. I'm ashamed to be in the rays of your reading eyes. I can't

*(secret words deleted years later, as he types this out)*

I sat down next to a man who had done some work. There are always such people around to illumine one's sloth. The modesty of this one was especially reproachful. His hands told me how lazy I am. His quietness told me how loud. His wrinkles told me how weak I am. His shoulders told me how proud.

I won't. I won't take another woman casually. Only when her beauty is manifest. Only when she strikes me with her juicy grace. Only when she comes forward and there is no doubt. She will not come forward now. There she is. That is part of her skin. I think it is the shadowy arc between her buttocks. I think it is her "green intelligence." I won't fuck in the Holy Land unless she is my True Wife. Surely this hateful one I leave behind is not my True Wife. And other such thoughts as I rode the sea

*(and other such thoughts that led him to this lousy kitchen table in the middle of the night with FM jazz and consolations of the diary, and her in the arms of youth, years later, as he types this out)*

Yorgo T. boarded the ship at Aegina, a cunt-struck landowner from this very island, home of the pistachio nut and superior pistachio ice-cream. I asked him if he had any news of Henrietta, an English inn-keeper of mutual acquaintance who had a sad reputation for biting into cocks, disinterested information of her existence being the mainstay of our accidental annual conversations. Yes, he had news, but not very pleasant news. She had come to Athens. She had contacted him. They had arranged a rendezvous but both had turned up at different times due to a misunderstanding of clocks. Some time later when he called her hotel he was informed that she was not physically capable of using the telephone. He summoned the hotel manager to the line and he was advised not to come to see her, it was not a pretty sight. Some weeks later he received a letter from Henrietta, postmarked London, with a depressing explanation. Apparently she had been badly tortured by three Japanese tourists behind a restaurant. This was the first conversation with Yorgo T. that I had enjoyed in a long time.

—Do you believe this preposterous story? I asked him. It was amazing how clear-brained I had become. Just a little sea between me and the creature of unbeauty and the world had begun to surface. He stuffed a cigarette into an ivory tube and pretended not to hear me. We sipped our ouzos, perfectly content, giving nothing, two civilized men.

—Why aren't you in Israel? he said, thinking he had me there.

—As a matter of fact that's exactly where I'm going.

—Really? Really? He stood up delighted.

—I'll go directly to the airport as soon as we dock. That's what I'm doing here.

—Bravo, he said. Really. Bravo. Bravo. Bravo. He seized both my hands in his and squeezed them with true enthusiasm and something like gratitude. Oh I'm so pleased, he said. Bravo. Bravo. Evidently I now represented certain old virtues which he cherished deeply. More than love of cunt did we have in common. We were the Shield, we were the Men Who Defended. My house, his house. My land, his land. Because of this we were granted cigarette holders, loneliness and the right to speak of women casually.

—You must. You must, he said.

—I know. I know. I felt humble and doomed. His eyes seemed to be shining at an honoured corpse. The degree of his admiration had now attracted more than several of our fellow passengers. These he commenced to address in Greek:

—This man is travelling to Israel to defend his country against his country's enemy. He leaves a well-appointed house, a woman and a child, all the comforts of his achievement. I wonder how many of

89

you, if you lived let us say in Holland or Sweden in similar circumstances, would sacrifice your security and come back here, if the threat arose, to fight against the Turk. Bravo, Leonard. Bravo. Bravo. Bravo.

With a contemptuous wave of the hand he sent the worms back to their private holes to reconsider their cowardice, and we embraced. I must be doing something really stupid, I said to myself, to make another man so happy.

# ANGELICA

Angelica stands by the sea
Anything I say is too loud for her mood
I will have to come back
a million years later
with the scalp of my old life
hanging from one hand


## ANGELICA

She went back to the beach to look for the room key which she thought she might have dropped there. I ran to tell her that the door was open. I stopped at the edge of the sand. The sun was going down. She had lied about the key to escape from the family. She stood in front of the sun. She had become pure attention. My heart was fouled with anxieties of the occasion. I fell to one knee remembering the feathered helmet and shield and how I had betrayed my calling, clinging to the glory of the investiture, my strength spent in boasting and lust while I embraced the alibi of the artist.

# THE NEXT ONE

Things are better in Milan.
Things are a lot better in Milan.
My adventure has sweetened.
I met a girl and a poet.
One of them was dead
          and one of them was alive.
The poet was from Peru
          and the girl was a doctor.
She was taking antibiotics.
I will never forget her.
She took me into a dark church
          consecrated to Mary.
Long live the horses and the candles.
The poet gave me back my spirit
          which I had lost in prayer.
He was a great man out of the civil war.
He said his death was in my hands
because I was the next one
          to explain the weakness of love.
The poet Cesar Vallejo
          who lies at the foot of his forehead.
Be with me now great warrior
whose strength depends solely
          on the favours of a woman.

# THE NEXT ONE

*from the original version of My Life in Art:*

I lost my tan in Italy and I got fat on pasta and the starch of loneliness. I must fast for forty days. Sabina wrote me from the temple in Germany. She said that the old books say you should fast once each year for the number of days corresponding to your age. She was on the eighth day of an intended twenty-eight-day fast. Also I neglected to twist my feet so the heart went crazy. I must phone Patricia who was so good to me. The line is busy.

# NO ONE WATCHING

Lie down. There's no one watching you. On numberless threads the snowflakes are pulled back into the night sky. The show is over. Tip out great handfuls of buttock. The girl has come.

## NO ONE WATCHING

*a marvellous night*
*a marvellous woman*
*they married in the winter*
*they parted in the spring*
*she threw her wedding ring*
*into the Lake of Decisions*
*she continued*
*he continued*
*they met again*
*in the south of France*
*she was living alone*
*but in great beauty*
*he appeared to her*
*as a toad*
*she chased him*
*out of the 18th century*
*he thinks of her all the time*
*but in the winter*
*he goes crazy*
*he walks up & down the room*
*singing Hank Williams*
*the police put tickets on his car*
*the snow removal people*
*cover it with snow*
*finally it is towed away*
*to a huge white field*
*of frozen dogs*

## THE EVENT

The event engrossed me.
A pigeon flew across the window.
The Chinese girl smiled.
I made my vows to her.
We would never fuck.
We would never speak.
We would never meet.
The unlimited grey afternoon
supported all its creatures evenly.

## *THE EVENT*

*Several versions of The Event appear in a minuscule (3½ x 2¼) Baberton Junior notebook purchased from a stationers on Wardour Street in London during the winter of 1972. I would not part with this little orange-covered notebook for anything less than one thousand dollars. That was a terrible lonely rainy winter.*
*One version is titled*
*EVENT IN A RESTAURANT ON WARDOUR STREET*
*and here we discover that the Chinese girl did not merely smile but*

The Chinese girl smiled
at the waiter

*Obviously his vanity prohibits him from preserving the object of her attention, and furthermore he is so pissed off by her "benign indifference" toward himself that he deletes her ornament*

A small round diamond barrette
twinkled in the black hair
it clasped above her temple

*In the same notebook we find a variation on the Three-Fold Refuge theme which is embraced by the half of mankind which bows to "the great god Bud," a somewhat Judaized version:*

I go for refuge to the Lord
I go for refuge to the Law
I go for refuge to the Congregation

*Do we find, perhaps, in the vows he makes to her, an echo of the Three-Fold Refuge? Also "the unlimited grey afternoon" is a filthy oriental idea, obsessed as they are with what is limited and what is not limited, or what is both limited and unlimited, or neither limited nor unlimited.*

Event engrossed me
Pigeon across window
Girl smiled waiter
Vows to her me:
Never fuck
Never speak
Never meet
Tables away I sit on grey afternoon
with her and all things
the content of my being

*It is still exquisite in translation.*

# THE JELLY

The moon is over the windmill. I sit here with a blanket around my shoulders. The daisies are all collapsed. It is very quiet. A dog is barking. I hope I can leave the garden soon. A clicking insect measures out a portion of the lightest breeze. Alexandra changed her name to Chandra, so many parts of her body and mind resembling the moon. I inhaled her essence yesterday afternoon when I walked near the shore where I first saw her breasts revealed. And who else visits me in a spinal chill. And moistens the eyes. They are gone now, many blonde faces. There is that bird that feeds on moonbeams, a kind of partridge. I think I could be clean again. I could live with you, beloved. You dance so gracefully with my head. And Chandra goes by lightly, silver and coughing, with the moon between her shoulders, stars attending each of her hardened nipples. It is truly quiet now. A wave bends me over the blue table, and a dream of the mountain rolling down over the roofs and the daisies. When can I be with you again. When can I put my hands in the blood. The moon begins sliding down the mountain toward the sea. Your nipple like a planet, ringed like Saturn. I will never forget you. It is years and I have not forgotten the kisses of our mouths. We are hidden behind our plans. Lenore, are you here. Dundi, untouchable as the other telephone. Over the daisies, across the lane, fifty feet away is the chapel of Agia Tichon. The prayers of others wash over me. I will defend the chapel. I have been placed at the foot of this heap of daisies to defend whatever is in my eyesight and under my nose. Now you may go to sleep with all your kindergarten pals. I cannot always be on my knees, swooning before the lord. I have to feed the swine. I have to sit on them. I have to come riding out of the moonlight and get the jelly from their feet.




## THE JELLY

*I got the jelly from their feet*
  *ya ya ya*
*I got the jelly from their feet*
  *ya ya ya*
*I got the jelly from their feet*
  *it's very thick*
  *it's very sweet*
*I got the jelly from their feet*
  *ya ya ya*

## YOU HAVE NO FORM

You have no form, you move among, yet do
not move, the relics of exhausted thought
of which you are not made, but which give world to
you, who are of nothing made, nothing wrought.
There you long for one who is not me, O
queen of no subject, newer than the morning,
more antique than first seed dropped below
the wash where you are called and Adam born.
And here, not your essence, not your absence
weds the emptiness which is never me,
though these motions and these formless events
are preparation for humanity,
and I get up to love and eat and kill
not by my own, but by our married will.


*YOU HAVE NO FORM*

*They should cast your cunt in chrome for the
radiator cap of a Buick.*

# MY DEAD DOG

I blew smoke rings into your alleged beauty, "alleged" because everyone believes it but you and me. On the other hand, if you turned up anytime this winter with your hair piled on top of your head like the Acropolis and other official wonders, I would get down on my knees just to honour the immense fiction of our understanding. O absent fiat of my dead dog, come back to this neutral holiday. I am drunk on everyone's defeat and full of self-congratulations to be a friend of the snow.

## THE DREAM

O I had such a wonderful dream, she said.
I dreamed you made love to me.
At last, he said to himself, the spirit
has taken up some of the heavy work.

# THE DREAM

*from the Notebooks of 1975:*

> She said, I had a wonderful dream. I dreamed you made love to me. It felt so good. She was happy for an hour or two. I was pleased to learn that the spirit has taken up some of the heavy work. That was the morning of the sixth day of a fast. I broke it that night. She cleared away more of the weeds and dried daisies and planted roses and grape-vine cuttings. There is no place for me back there.

*He refers to the incident again in the Notebooks of 1977:*

> It was an unexpected (although long overdue) justification of my heavy and reluctant investment in meditation, fasting, dismal prayer, and holy conversation.

> I felt a lot like Atlas when he was tapped on the shoulder by an hydraulic jack.

*from a Diary Tape of 1978:*

> I was a fool to be bitter or make light of it. The marriage <u>had</u> moved to another realm but I was not quick enough to follow it. I couldn't appreciate her work in the garden. I had come to depend too much on the weeds.

## A MODEST GIFT

It was a modest gift
Five-foot-eight in the Age of Dwarfs
Those nostalgic for the future
those who mourned the ancient excellence
did right to ignore me
But you deluded darling
you died in captivity
believing you'd surrounded a poet

## *A MODEST GIFT*

*I don't think this should be viewed exclusively as the usual Tolstovian resentment of the woman's constant presence. It is also the old interior quarrel (upon which the universe is sustained) of the limited vs. the unlimited. The poet, by naming himself such, is condemned to the suffocating captivity of a conceptual existence instead of O GOD MY HEART IS YOURS.*

*The original version is found in a sturdy Swedish notebook, the Atlanta Radio-Serie/ A 2202-6/ 120 BL. It was written sometime in 1973 at the Bayshore Inn in Vancouver. The variation is*

As for you poor deluded darling

*The piece is immediately preceded by, and may even be part of, a number of lines which amount to nothing more or less than a parody on the metaphysic of polarity, an extremely ugly parody to my way of thinking:*

I am ———————   ——————*
I walk on my hands
I live upside down
to be ready for your cunt
in attitudes you love
I was sold down
the long milky rivers of your skin
I went over the Falls
Your fur is my only hello
Other greetings are the vomit
of the unrequited world
Fuck the tractor
            on my astral legs
I stretch them whole and hairy
Hello hello my love
the low heavens of Vancouver
lie down on us
as we enter the earth
            for the last time
the lips of speech and silence
drink each other dry

*Identity withheld to protect the innocent

105

# THE KWIKANICE CAFÉ

Nobody looking good enough to fuck,
is that it,
failed saint of the Kwikanice Café?
Sitting on your jacked-off tool,
no energy to bless the carousel?
Make your way to where I am,
restless sperm,
you are the ghost of love
and I am love itself.

## THE KWIKANICE CAFÉ

*That's how it will come, your forgiveness. You will be sitting at the kitchen table, maybe listening to the radio, Charlebois singing about the end of summer, and the forgotten prayer for forgiveness which has sunk into the heart far beneath your shame, it will be answered; this world, your proper home, will come back, you will know that you have been forgiven. When the content of your useless heart is nothing but a prayer for forgiveness, a prayer that has been forgotten, that is raging like a cell disease beneath your artificial health*

Make your way to where I am
restless sperm
you are the ghost of love
I am love itself

*Where is your beauty now, Lord of Sorrows? Where is your club foot, your boot like a huge black telephone? Where is your black blouse and your throat of young ropes? Where are your many nipples, O Mother of Cats, your inventions of anger, your refusals that have come loose like a rattle of doves? Where is the thin moustache of your iron will and your fine nib of parentheses?*

*Now there is no one waiting to be loved, or to be touched first, no one waiting in the fluted lighthouse for his mind to change. Dissolved like a horn into the thigh, dissolved like a moth into the harbour's silver diagram, like a dart into Steven's extra body*

*we have entered the pile of chairs that ended The Last Supper*

*Where is your beauty now, Lord of Sorrows, streaming toward the blaze of innocence like a windshield made of ice*

107

## I LIKE THE WAY YOU OPPOSED ME

I like the way you opposed me when you thought I had fallen into silence. You were so happy that I had nothing to teach you, and nobody spoke of my exploits. All this depended on a curious belief of yours that there was only one stage, and you had been waiting for my piece to end, feeling so ripe and swollen for the spot. And here I am again, with the news of another freedom, just when yours was selling well and the competition was under control. You might like to know what my wife said to me upstairs. She's wearing her wine bikini, she's rather attractive, you know, in spite of her shaved head which was the idea of your Central Committee. She said, Leonard, whenever you leave the room an orange bird comes to the window.

## I LIKE THE WAY YOU OPPOSED ME

I like the way you...

> *You appear. Whether or not he likes you is a matter for the beasts of truth.*

You were so happy that I had nothing to teach you...

> *That is why he cannot speak in this line.*

All this depended...

> *The only charity here is the "one stage" which includes both of you. The rest is the suffering of a conditioned, dependent and particular vision. But this suffering is swollen and cannot maintain itself.*

And here I am again...

> *It is pleasant to have him born again. That breeze comes right off the ocean.*

You might like to know what my wife...

> *This is the same as the above. His wife appears. He is born with his wife. You have begun to dissolve.*

She's wearing her wine bikini...

> *This world of staircases and bikinis is a real world and we are at home in it. He is wearing her wine bikini and she is manifesting his luminous skull. All the Russias are invited to appear in the midst of their desire.*

She said, Leonard, whenever you leave the room...

> *You leave the room. You disappear. There is no you. An orange bird unifies the world. Even the beasts of truth are fed. Even the monster of peace takes off his crown.*

## BESIDE MY SON

I lay beside my sleeping son.
He was not a child now.
A dream radiated from his lips.
He was unusually good company.

## BESIDE MY SON

*May you bless the union of your mother and father*
*May you discard easily the husks of my thought*
*May you stand on my dead body*

# SHE HAS GIVEN ME THE BULLET

Just after sunset
waves creeping up to our toes
my wife said: I have everything I want
I looked down at her hair
as she snuggled against my shoulder like a rifle-butt
Toward the horizon
mist fumed out of the water changing clearly
into the eternal shapes of comfort and ordeal
I will bring these down, I said to myself,
she has given me the bullet

## SHE HAS GIVEN ME THE BULLET

There is the bullet but there is no death. There is the mist but there is no death. There is the embrace but there is no death. There is the sunset but there is no death. There is the rotting and the hatred and the ambition but there is no death. There is no death in this book and therefore it is a lie.

THE GOOD FIGHT

If only she'd call me Mister again
If only my genitals didn't float
When I relaxed in the bath
And we both looked down and we both agreed
It's stupid to be a man
Don't tell my mother I've become
The appendix of a full-grown woman
I'm made of her I'm useless to her
I'm something gouged out with her beauty
I'm the shape of her perfume
I'm the chime of wire hangers
That she took her clothes down from
When I made her strong and angry
With the subtlest insults I could devise
And still she would not fall
And I knew for certain
She was the Magnum Opus of my middle-age

*THE GOOD FIGHT*

*The twenty-third verse of the third chapter of Pirke Aboth (Sayings of the Fathers), a short tractate of the Mishmah:*

Rabbi Eleazar Hisma said: Offerings of birds and purifications of women, these, yea these, are the essential precepts. Astronomy and geometry are but the fringes of wisdom.

114

"What are here translated 'offerings of birds' and 'purifications of women,' refer to the offerings brought by women after childbirth and for reasons arising out of the monthly periods. To explain them fully would need a minute knowledge of halachah and is not necessary for the present purpose. The point is that they are declared to be the very essence of the Torah."

(R. Travers Herford's Commentary)

*Go beyond his clumsy confession to the infuriating presumptions of the Rabbi. The function of birth or appearing is the proper concern for the creatures on the crust of this star. We have all appeared here together. Creation and menstruation, birth and the birth from which nothing appears, these are the awesome limits of our existence here. Also, nothing happens when you fuck yourself.*

*When will we collaborate again, men and women, to establish a measure for our mighty and different energies? When will we speak frankly again about our insane and homicidal appetites? We are each other's Mystery. This Mystery will not yield to violence or dissection. Please don't start singing.*

Lost in the floodtides of fashion
O please bring her back to the captain
Who steers by the star of her wisdom
Forever above and beyond him

*When Jerusalem has been dissolved the Temple will arise in every heart where men will study the art of naming and women will focus the powers of life and death, all in the great clarity of understanding that the Lord is One. This is the disgusting thrust of a Sunday School mind.*

# THE DOVE

I saw the dove come down, the dove with the green twig, the childish dove out of the storm and flood. It came toward me in the style of the Holy Spirit descending. I had been sitting in a café for twenty-five years waiting for this vision. It hovered over the great quarrel. I surrendered to the iron laws of the moral universe which make a boredom out of everything desired. Do not surrender, said the dove. I have come to make a nest in your shoe. I want your step to be light.

# THE DOVE

*from the blue-spined Italian Notebook, summer of 1975:*

> Who is it, who is it
> who leaves dust on the glass
> who moves the petals
> from the stem to the table
> One afternoon of rain in Rome
> I decided to surrender
> to the one who kept my love from me

Then I began to live in Rome with Patricia. She was
very good to me. I liked her dog. This was in the old
part of town. She was like me. She knew the code.

> I saw the dove come down
> over the heads of the people
> over the police and the people
> over the old stones
> and the living congregations
> under the arches and towers
> I saw the dove with the green twig
> the childish dove
> out of the storm and the flood
> pure and undivided still
> in the world of sun and rain
> Green was the twig
> and white was the wing
> I saw the dove come down
> to live under my feet
> to live in the stone
> the foundation of

Tonight Patricia looks like everyone. She looks like
Ava Gardner. She looks like Sheila who died of

117

cancer. She looks like my cousin Lyon. She loves her dog. She says her dog loves me. He wants my biscuit. She wears a long dress. Wisps of hair are free. It's okay she says. She gives me something made with oranges, a cookie. The dog weeps for it. I give part of it to the dog. My life in art continues.

Drinking every day. C & W singer trying to forget you. Your dead field. Your huge demand. Vieux Bordeaux in a green glass from Afghanistan.

> I see the dove. It hates you.
> It hurls a gate down on you,
> a black gate with iron spikes

Around her neck Patricia wears the anchor, cross and heart. The sun comes out and she puts on her sunglasses. We may have to take off our sweaters. I will slowly fall in love with her. There is no hurry. There is nothing bitter. I will become her dog. We are waiting for the bill.

Just now I actually saw two doves come down toward me in the style of the Holy Spirit descending, light behind the tail feathers and the wings. I have been sitting in a cafe for twenty-five years waiting for this vision. I surrender to the iron laws of the moral universe, which make a boredom out of everything desired. I will go back to my dark companion. I don't think I will. One of these days I'm going to let my hair go curly. The perfect woman loves that kind of hair.

*Now, your sneer still bright and fresh, go back and read THE DOVE.*

# THE ROSE

I was never bothered by the rose. Some people talk about it all the time. It fades, it blooms. They see it in visions, they have it, they miss it. I made some small efforts to worry about the rose but they never amounted to much. I don't think you should do those things to a flower. They don't exist anyhow. The garden doesn't exist either. Believe me, these things stand in the way. I was with a man when he actually saw the rose. He said his mother was standing at the centre of it. I went to war with the rose on my banner but I didn't fight very well. The rose has never eluded me. It's the most natural thing to see it burning in the air in front of me like a little fire in the middle of a sheet of paper, a bright hole with blackened edges. Sometimes it floats over my right shoulder like a red umbrella. It has four green leaves at the cardinal points. It claims to sponsor these lines. It is a very modest claim but it stands in the way. It was granted to me to discard the authority of the rose. Between the cheeks it still has its terrors. These are harmless conventions. I smell the fragrance. It has even filled up my car on the highway far from any flower bed. I can feel the thorns if I want to move my hand that carelessly. All this is perfectly natural. Sometimes the rose occupies the opening of the far end of a tunnel. I never allow this to dignify my approach. They are continually hovering in windows and other apertures which attract light or desire. They are usually perceived one at a time and while the petals may undulate the centre is still. I never greet the rose and I never ask it to represent an idea or a woman. I find this stands in the way. Everywhere I discover men speaking to the rose. It does not improve their ordinary conversation. Then there is the wound like a rose. This is a particularly nauseating conception. The rose-wound. The petals are made of blood and the energy is made of pain. One of these dwells under my white shirt. There are three roses in my room right now and another trying to establish me as its centre. These are interfering dreams. Don't trouble yourself to brush them aside. You wouldn't know how to do it anyway, and they would probably install themselves on the floor near your feet in theatrical attitudes of agony and neglect.

# THE ROSE

*Years later (1977), in the driveway of a
Brentwood ranch-house, weakened by Zen meditation
and a faultless woman, he allows The Rose to manifest.
The Rose tries to interfere with him. He protects his
haunches by leaning against the fender of an antique
Mercedes, and to gather his resistances, he improvises a
song:*

It's been hard since I left The Garden
I don't feel so good in my clothes
But I'm not shaking hands with The Warden
And I'm not going back to The Rose

I miss the vice of a man like Christ
And there's too many Arthur Rimbauds
But I'm not going back to Paradise
And I'm not going back to The Rose

*The Rose begins to discorporate. He rushes
toward it. The delivery man from the Health Food Dairy
finds him standing beside the bougainvilia, his eyes
closed, kissing the air.*

121

## ANOTHER MAN'S WOMAN

Now in the form of another man's woman.
Sitting at our table.
Holding her cup in the morning light.
Saying: Into your life I will tangle one
whom you cannot approach
in order that you may refine your love for me.
Look at my beauty now.

## ANOTHER MAN'S WOMAN

*from the Notebooks of 1973:*

so you come to me now
in the form of one I cannot approach
    tired of your cloak of light
    and your filmy lakeside memorial
I see you emerge from numbers of people
like moon out of scarves of cloud
but the Iron Guard marching between us

So you come to me now in the form of one whom I cannot approach. Taking the cloak of flesh. Sitting at our table. Holding the cup in the morning light. She serves you innocently. You say to me in the midst of my envy: Look at my beauty now. I am perfect still. You cannot touch me. I am as distant from you as I was before.

    O love you stayed away from me so long as I scraped the sides of my old vision for remnants of your presence
    Now in the form of a veiled girl
    now in the rush of my heart
the Iron Guard marching between us
With your sweater and your coffee and your cigarette and your plans for the morning

123

## ST. FRANCIS

Blue curtains in the neighbour's outhouse. Almond blossoms over a roof. A southerly breeze spills the daisies. A hummingbird bounces on a membrane of air. A foot below the butterfly its shadow blows across a rock. All this looked a lot more interesting ten years ago on acid, when I addressed the daisies in a style made popular by St. Francis. Some time later I visited his tomb. I took away some small metal birds blessed by the Abbot. It was a peaceful place. I did feel peaceful beside his powder. Dare I say he welcomed me? It's true! It's true! I feel his hand on my shoulder.

## ST. FRANCIS

*Beware of what comes out of Montreal, especially during the winter. It is a force corrosive to all human institutions. It will bring everything down. It will defeat itself. It will establish the wilderness in which the Brightness will manifest again.*

*We who belong to this city have never left The Church. The Jews are in The Church as they are in the snow. The most violent atheist radical defectors from le Parti Québécois are in The Church. Every style in Montreal is the style of The Church. The winter is in The Church. The Sun Life Building is in The Church. Long ago the Catholic Church became a pebble beside the rock on which The Church was founded. The Church has used the winter to break us and now that we are broken we are going to pull down your pride. The pride of Canada and the pride of Quebec, the pride of the left and the pride of the right, the pride of muscle and the pride of heart, the insane pride of your particular vision will swell and explode because you have all dared to think of killing people. The Church despises your tiny works of death and The Church declares that EVERY MAN, WOMAN AND CHILD IS PROTECTED.*

*Everyone knows that The Church is in Montreal. St. Francis is one of many who came through the snow to repair it, or rather, to repair the appearance of its ruin. Now The Church begins the militant phase: every idea of salvation withers in the Brightness of this blaze.*

# THE DRAWING

I drew a number of buildings. I put in every window, every shutter, every balcony. I put flowers where they were and people behind the glass, and details of the pillars and the statuary. Try to talk, I said to myself. A Madonna and Child was painted on one of the walls. I put that in. Put in the dove descending. Put a wafer in her beak. Put in the Hammer and Sickle. Put in the aerials and the ghosts among them raising their arms. Put in the muscles of the clouds. What colour are your eyes? Sometimes hazel, sometimes green. Put in Patricia's eyes. Put the Lord of Indecision in one of the alleys. Put the Lord of Failure there. Put the Idols of Desire beside the fountain. Then come back and talk to me, where your comfort is, where your refuge is.

# THE DRAWING

*from the corrasable pages of August 1976:*

> and even mighty History
> with his bells and butcher dress
> comes meekly to your solitude
> his mutiny to confess

*on a sheet of the Robertson Parkway Ramada Inn stationery:*

> you looked for life and death in the bodies
> which I gave you, finding only putrescence and
> decay. I took life and death out of the world
> because you did not come to me. If you starve
> for life and death you may come to me

*from the small Montreal notebook of 1954:*

> Perfect my twisted ways
> one cries at last at last one cries
> when neighbours do not matter
> or the love one sleeps beside

> One cries at last his faith hewn down
> by partial journeys into love
> O ruins of blind enterprise
> O coward shortened pilgrimage

# O WIFE UNMASKED

O wife unmasked
O body of my plunder
foundation of my waiting
unforgivable
and continually alluring
Some witness loves you
as you blunder through
the webs of my sleeping spirit
Some witness points at our bed
like a monument to romance and song
and gets another crowd to wonder
O juices and fragrance
and inhospitable warmth
O last remains of dignity
O shadow brood of hatred love remorse
O ribbons and trajectories
annulling distances
O wires rays and chains
What channels of intense air
trembling to a signal
What alloys of eyesore and starlight
What sad bureaucracy of luck
to be with you and you alone
muddling through the Day of Judgement

## O WIFE UNMASKED

*Claustrophobia! Bullshit! Air! Air! Give us air!*
*Is there an antidote to this mustard gas of domestic*
*spiritism?*
*Can we ever recover that beach at Molivos when*

the wave sank back
the head rolled on the beach
I lifted it and let it down
on my torn neck
I looked at the sea and the night
out of the eyes
of one who gave himself
to the knives of drunken love
so calm to know I was at last
YOUR COMPLETED MONSTER, LORD

*or the deep-throated birds in the small courtyard, the*
*camp bed, the freedom of the suede-soft White Notebook*
*of 1971*

there he goes
    with his fear of death
there he goes
    with his pot belly
past the small cafés
on the 21st of April Street
    there he goes
accompanied by music
from the movie
    and don't describe the trees
don't bother to mention the stars
    there he goes
his own man at last

past the pebble beach
past the ones he did not speak to
the ones he did not sleep with
        you remember him perhaps
as an admirer of cats
a vessel of monstrous longing
an elegiac connoisseur of islands
there he goes
        with his mind on cunt
        on cunt only
        heart money attention talent art
tuned entirely to cunt
and that's where he's going
exactly where he's going
a beautiful spectacle
a man who knows where he's going

        *Can we put down that wedding ring from
Jerusalem, the one with the heavy little silver house built
on it? Can we recover*

the course that jerks her upward
seized prisoner of the stars
her buttocks relax in my hands
like meat freshly killed

## THE WINDOW

A blonde boy wearing thick glasses just looked in my window, or rather at my window, for he used it as a mirror in which he confirmed his coiffure and his expression. I was afraid he might catch sight of me behind his reflection but he quit his work unaware of the self-centred host of this sunken room, and I did not have to confront him in the midst of his vanity.

## *THE WINDOW*

*This is the working of Mercy.*

# THE RADIO

Put on the radio. Light up a cigarette. You are a normal citizen. Fiddle among the stations. Find a good tune. Not the opera. Not the static. Not the passionate Arab violins. Not the armour-plated symphony. Not the shy French rhymer of birds and boats. Turn off the radio. You can hear the wind again. Light up another cigarette. Lean forward. Jiggle your knees. Your groin isn't giving you any trouble. You are not aching with desire. Try the radio. The Greek is all right. It's midnight now. The governments are speaking. They are speaking in curious regionless accents. What sad religions they want us to believe. They will speak all night, slowly and deliberately, as if their patience and their electricity were inexhaustible. They will not wake up your wife and bring her smiling into the room all warm to say, "I had a dream. We were married under a wave. The child is awake." I won't speak to you until you make yourself quiet. Half your life I have waited for you like this with my arms folded, turned away from you. Touch your buttocks. Lean forward. Jiggle your knees. No cigarette? No radio? No adult at command of his career? Just the frightened creature with nothing to teach?


## THE RADIO

*from the Final Revision of My Life in Art:*

Here is the promised land. It looks like the radio you can't listen to. It looks like your fly undone and your stomach hanging out. It looks like your unworked

132

hands. It looks like the mind perceived by the mind, a barren shit-box. It looks like your judgement of me

You are far from it. You have not even been granted a glimpse from Pisgah. It looks like your thinking elbows. It looks like the filter cigarette. It looks like the food-drugged tree of blood. It looks like your body. It looks like the swelling of hatred. It looks like peace in the house

Let the house fall down. Let water through the concrete and into the beams. Let weeds unbalance the steps. Let water through the wall. And don't let it shine anymore. Don't let it be a harbour anymore. And break the idol of love

(Homage to the Government

There is a true "hospital" not far from here. The "doctor" is wearing yellow rubber gloves purchased by himself at a hardware store. It is his own idea. Two female "nurses" wheel an electric machine into the room where the "patient" is secured to the "bed." The "nurses" fold back the top sheet. The bottom sheet is rubber. The "doctor" seizes the "testicles" of the "patient" and twists them hard, saying: How are we getting along today? The "patient" stares out of his round "eyes." His mouth is taped. The "nurses" attach "wires" to "shaved places" on his "skull")

This is not my voice. This is my voice. This isn't. She is beautiful half the time. She is a description. She has black hair. She has bad skin. She is a description. You wrestle with an angel. She surprises you with her buttocks. I made her for you out of everything you hate. I did this for no reason. You are busy with your idols. Now your idol is unreason. As if unreason represents me. As if it doesn't

133

# THE IDOLS OF THE LORD

Be sweet to me
    I sing to you
Be severe
    I give you laws
Clap your hands
    I let you dance
This is an idol of the lord

Birds are singing
    Day beginning
People breathing frankincense
Bring me
    pen and paper now
I have to write
    His Name again
This is an idol of the lord

What holy is
I do not know
    or what you want
with me below
Your Name disgraced
    by what you make
Your Name despised
    by such as us
All is holy
    All is foul
This is an idol of the lord

Woman in
    an open dress

Press her nipples
　　on my wax
Make her ask
　　me for release
When I'm before you
　　on my knees
The ova ships
　　the semen hoards
by arms embraced
　　by vows ignored
This is an idol of the lord

Sponsoring boredom
　　Spiriting cock
Mounting panic
　　Moistening cunt
Looking at you
　　with small birds' eyes
Slipping panties
　　over your face
I am your back
　　I am your front
Body is holy
　　Mind is a toy
On seas of thought
　　or matter's shore
Divide my world
　　from skin to core
or make it one
　　as it was before
Overthrow me
　　one more time
This decision
　　this decision
is an idol of the lord

## THE IDOLS OF THE LORD

*first verse:*

Your concept of mechanical reciprocity — does it work? Are you sure it doesn't? Why did you kneel down to this clanking old cast-iron cream separator?

*second verse:*

Even Abulafia lost his place in Paradise because of this.

*third verse:*

The agnostic's pride, his tiny secret confession of resentment, his marrano faith in ultimate balance — utterly rejected!

*fourth verse:*

This book, the romantic tantra, the mating of Adam and Eve in the venereal Kabala, the Korean flag — utterly rejected!

*fifth verse:*

including your crude voodoo milkshake of semen and menstrual blood
including the ninety-day disclaimer
including the apotheosis of all your pursed lips
including the vanity of the hunt
including the excuse of shock treatments
including what I dare not say about Dachau and New York

THOU SHALT HAVE NO OTHER GODS BEFORE ME

## YOUR DEATH

You are a dead man
writing me a letter
Your sunglasses are beside you
on the square table
on the green felt
You write carefully
sentence after sentence
to make your meaning clear
The meaning is
that you are dead
dead with hope
dead with spring
dead with the blurred hummingbird
dead with the longing
to shine again
in details of the past
And you are tied to your death
with hope
with the hope of sliding out
from under your death
and then to stand
and brandish a scar
in the palm of your hand
like an invitation to the next ordeal
You pass the night
with the source of your death
trying to praise it
trying to sell it
trying to touch it
Your death is fine with me
It has given you
the beautiful head you wanted

the face with good lines
and even though
you cannot inhabit this skull
I can and I do
and I thank you
for the deep heroism
of your useless correspondence.

## YOUR DEATH

*Ever since the rocks and trees began to approach me with pleasant greetings I have thought very little about how you would receive my letters. Even though your perception of my death is imperfect, I am happy that you like my face, and that you appreciate this little drama at the table. I had forgotten that you can be generous. I am surprised and pleased. It is Mozart's birthday today. But you know that. And you know about the blemish and the swollen belly. It is only my blessing that you do not know, and still you say Amen. "Greater is he that answers Amen than he that says the blessing."*

PETITIONS


       The blind man loves you with his eyes, the deaf man with his music. The hospital, the battlefield, the torture room, serve you with numberless petitions. On this most ordinary night, so bearable, so plentiful in grave distractions, touch this worthless ink, this work of shame. Inform me from the great height of your beauty.


*PETITIONS*

Inform me from the great height of your beauty.
       *I discovered the genesis of this lovely melody on pages 2-4 of the Challenge Duplicate Book, scribbled in Germany sometime during the winter of 1972:*

My official life
  has become extensive
First of all
  I only sing official songs
at official concerts
  and I play
my official Ramirez guitar
for official audiences
  In Stockholm a female official
serving drinks at the Crazy Horse
porno bar infected me
with a disease
diagnosed officially as gonoreahia (sic)
cured by an official and monstrous
  needle in Berlin
My phone conversations are all official
even the most casual
Iris is officially unavailable
She told me that at the jukebox
which was undergoing my official
  inspection
Her beauty was official blonde Botticelli
emerging among the pizzas in Munich
on my official visit to the student section

*The "official" song is abandoned here at the
bottom of page 2 (unlined). On page 4 (unlined) we find
the articulation of the "seed desire" which is the energy
behind the original entry and its evolution into
PETITIONS:*

Only to have Iris
smile on me
from the great height
of her beauty

141

# THE LANGUAGE OF LOVE

If I wasn't a vegetarian I'd eat steak now. I'd help you fuck yourself if I wasn't celibate. So listen, hard-core mourning boy, who cannot make peace with the language of love, listen to one who has grown ugly in the service of the Lord, who loves the snow in his back yard more than his infant son, listen before you steal another line or woman. This is made of poetry. My most random conversation with a snowflake is made of poetry. This is where I roll and swear like those shit-speech bullies who made you turn away and ruined your ear for music. This is my chaste winter meditation. Steal only what is your own from the store-room universal. Avoid fingerprints and snowflakes, there is only one of each. At this very moment you are in the hands of a master who wants to silence you. Speak up, speak up, ambitious lad, there is a limit to my compassion.

*This is the language of love, but the language spoken in lower worlds, among the citizens of the broken vessels. Nevertheless, wheels appear and turn, and creatures are moved from here to there. It is a garbled language, the letters weak and badly formed, the parchment stained with excrement; however, we are certain, there is no doubt that it derives from the great formula of letters, formed by a voice, impressed upon the air, and set in the mouth in five places, namely:*

*male and female created He them*

*Last night, while my daughter was sleeping in the room with the blue carpet from the Main, and my son was sleeping in my own bed, Lilith appeared to me. She has never given me up. As usual, I could not resist her. It was close enough to the full moon for me to receive a blemish. I received it in two places.*

*This morning, after taking the children to school, I drove down to the Avis garage to have snow tires put on the Datsun. They were amazed that I had been driving all winter without them (it is now the end of January). My power extends no further, but I am grateful for the huge and terrible safety with which He has so far surrounded me. And so it goes, the letters weaker and weaker, the distortions more grotesque, further and further from the voice, deeper and deeper in the Exile.*

*And now it comes to pass, that into this Exile, already swollen with men in their states of disease, their soiled and useless laws, their menstrual songs, their monstrous ideals — a place is cleared beside the filths of masculinity, and women are welcomed into the Exile.*

143

## SPEECH TO MY OLD FRIEND

Speech to my old friend. Good evening. The park is lovely tonight. The lilacs are in bloom. We are surrounded by the landmarks of our childhood. The goldfish shudder among the weeds. The swings are still. It is a pleasant puzzle to tell the moon from the lamplights on the surface of the pond. How did we get so far apart? Why did we let religion and ambition kill our friendship?

## SPEECH TO MY OLD FRIEND

> *On the other side of the coin, we have the entry of July 20, 1972, in the Challenge Duplicate Book:*

All you pretty sailors
    don't interest me no more
I got a man in Montreal
    who loves his welfare whore

With that finger out of heaven
    Michel Angelo produced
he revives my peanut brain
    long gone and overused

He has a tiny treasure
    that he spends on both of us
I love my unemployment
    He loves his Lazarus

Goodnight, goodnight you evil ones
    May you rest at last
There is a happy ending
    to all the bloody past

> *Surely this is the most elaborate closet that has ever been opened from the inside! In addition, we can examine, but not too closely, the journal entry of*

**January 6, 1970**

forgive me for tightening my asshole
against thee

## THE VISIT

So here you are again, ugly and glowing, like charcoal shit. You stand in the doorway, you flood the doorway with red waves of anger. You want to know what the matter is. Why don't I serve you anymore. You piece of shit. You actually came to ask me that. Your thighs are shapely and white but your huge mask of anger drips over them. You are top heavy. There are cinders in the air, pieces of carbon paper, old negatives. You step forward, ridiculous in your anger costume, like the kike you are, trying to imitate some noble motions of sacred dance. Don't try to smile. As if to say: forget it. I won't forget it. You are not harmless. I know your clumsy kike disguise. The helpless kike disguise. You mean I'm going to have to stay with you, line after line. Saying that, you leave; your buttocks beautiful as when first we met and I followed you into the fire. Thanks for the visit, you ugly bitch. I'll have to scrap this room for an hour or two. Not even a glance at my genitals, you useless bitch. But yesterday your spirit hand came through the foam just the way I like it. You learned by watching me. I found one thing in you to praise and on this pebble I built my fortress of love.

146

*THE VISIT*

>*It is so peaceful here with our ordinary life broken and her raw love in my spine.*

*THE VISIT*

>*It is so lovely in here. I could almost swoon. The heart might open. It was simple. I came inside. It's a place to breathe. It's cool and pleasant in here. I know the man who lives in this cabin. He told me to write this down. He was sitting in that chair a week ago. Why doesn't my chest explode. Why don't I burst out crying. I loved your hairy legs down by the waterfall. I have a woman's body and you have a man's body. We should sort this out in a tight embrace. You strong-smiling wrestler. You tried to start a fight down by the waterfall. That stream was too cold to fall in. O I did stare at your man's legs. The ladybugs were everywhere. You still want to fight me. Your knees are bent and your arms stretch out. O finely muscled spirit. Your laughter makes your eyes deep. You circle me. You're ready to spring. Why don't you spring. Somewhere in the flurry can I astonish you. O strong girl. O strong embracer. How brave you make the sunlight. I drink from your hands. I lie under your chin. Your belly is a pool for your muscles to plunge in, a pool at night with our bodies sorted and fresh*

147

# THE PLAN

The plan to marry her in Jerusalem with
Yemenite ornaments. The plan to be the man in this
wild garden. The plan to undo famine with the notion
of the Total Fast. The plan to lead through influence.
The plan to document these daisies. The plan to fish
every morning with Donald. The plan to sit an hour
each day with Anthony. The plan to go on the road
again. The plan of money and fast bodies. The plan to
return to dignity through the use of old clothes. The
plan of crossing to the other shore, landing safely on
the other shore. The plan of being street father to the
young writers in Montreal, using the harsh style. The
miserable plan of the invisible temple, a ceremony
with Asher. The plan to visit Egypt in homage to the
great woman's voice. The plan to study power in Ot-
tawa. The plan to overthrow my life with fresh love.
The plan to live with Roshi and serve him in the clean
drunk life. The plan to fall in love with my dark com-
panion, to see her beauty plain in the sweat of lawful
lust. The plan to teach my son that there is no light in
this world. The plan to follow my true song no matter
where. The plan to honour Henry M. and Mark P., the
great mad spirits who tempt me with their gratitude.
The plan to prevent the man from beating the horse.
The plan to heed the counsel of that man on the street
in San Francisco who put his finger to his lips as he
passed me. The plan to be strong ordinary muscular
and simple. The plan to say the daisies are shoulder
high on the very day that the description obtains, or to
adjust this description to other high demands. The plan
to make my face noble and attractive through hard
work and brave decisions. The plan for my body. The

plan to greet Steve S. in the highest ritual. A plan to be the seed. A plan to give up. A plan to assume the friendship of the lizards and the nettles. A plan to sing to the Mexican gardeners if I ever go back. The plan to be thin and fast and kind. My plan for you. My throne for you. My cunning toward God. There is a cat to my left, just hidden at the edge of the daisies, moving clumsily. Is this cat injured or is this cat about to give birth. The plan to escape. The plan not to witness.

## THE PLAN

*Every one of these plans was studied, materialized and followed. I married her in Jerusalem but I should not have allowed her to be circumcised by the old Nubian nurse. In the expanding desert of western Ethiopia I taught a simple Scientology exercise to the starving tribesmen. Soon they were gazing into each other's eyes, their hunger forgotten. I made myself immensely attractive by sucking in my cheeks, and many followed me. I wrote the Final Revision of My Life in Art. So now you know the truth, and when you are broken down enough, you will appreciate it. You will not feel so superior to those who kill in the name of Jesus Christ. You will not study so carefully the conflict between State and Society in Eastern Europe. Your sideburns will grow long and curl at length but the Jews will still despise you. You will not depend on the floor to receive your boots and you will not depend on your beard to be victimized. You will crawl without bending your knees. You will sing without parting your false grey lips. You will be thrown back. You will fall against me. And I, who could not heal myself, I will heal you. I am the Canadian and I am the French-Canadian. I am the Acadian. I am the smoke of Quebec and the kilt of Mt. Royal. I am the subtlest germ of the Quebecois and I am the core for the pores of snow. I have defeated all your plans with the weightless carcass of a summer fly. The one who comes after me has a clear field.*

## SACRIFICE

O Lord what shall I sacrifice to thee
the coins of lust that are my poverty
or can I place impatience on the fire
or can I make a fragrance of desire
I have no flawless dove to set ablaze
I have no silence, have no songs of praise
The burden of my heart I cannot lift
to burn it in your furnace as a gift
O lord I cannot speak I cannot hear
Your temple and your altar disappear
and only in my genitals you stir
and only in the purse beneath the fur
Dark ignorance and then unbidden peace
O murdered heart that sets my heart at ease
You take this joyless yearning to be free
You say it is acceptable to thee

*SACRIFICE*

*This is the working of Mercy.*

## I THINK YOU LIKE IT RAW

You do not seem to love my pious moods, you disdain my formal meditation, but when I come home with the smell of a new woman in my gums, and, after making love to my dark companion, while she sleeps, masturbating with the fond recollection of the two of us eating Joleen, you arrive gently to be with me at the bar of the Rainbow on Stanley Street, only pulling back a little as I write this down.


## *I THINK YOU LIKE IT RAW*

*That was the night of July 26, 1972.*
*You deceived me that night in your disguise of peace.*
*Look where I am now.*
*My dark companion lost*
 *for whose company I ache.*
*My children entering the strangerhood.*
*Your forms are immaculate.*
*Behind the mask of grief*
 *you bend me to the table.*
*Your idols perfect*
 *in all that they so thoroughly deny.*
*Far into the night*
 *you continue to manifest as her absence.*

I won't let you sit around drinking tea with us while I send my passionate decibels out to Monica. It might cause an erection unto you and the consequent increase of Lilith's brood, if you know what I mean, if you're up on who she is. You will have to go home like the rest of us. This is not a singles bar. There is no premium on the high stepper here.

Lilith and the grotesque issue of her womb, they suck at me all the time. They ate my brain this afternoon. They are hungry to augment their vile family. They caused me to set Monica before me at this desk and she showed me her thighs all laid out for a feast and she closed her dressing gown, opened it, closed it, what a commotion of fragrance she fanned upwards. I had to smoke a cigarette. I had to take a bath, which is a complicated procedure under the primitive circumstances of my life on this island, a condition I hopefully established to attract an inner purity.

Ah, you're back at last. I don't like to see you on the streets. I hope you're having a pleasant evening. I hope it's going well, the poker game or the conversation. I have the radio on but I can still hear the wind. I had a trumpet concerto for a while but it was gradually overwhelmed by Radio Moscow. I've been reasonable as you can see. I built an incinerator out of rocks today and I burned some trash. I saw my wife reading a cookbook in bed. I practise the arts of peace.

A surrendering kiss might rescue the night, but could such a kiss be formed by or accepted from the lips and teeth of one's mate? This is the monastery of marriage. This is my chaste reflection. This is when I find your scorn most attractive, O golem of service and monotony, posing once again your famous boring question: Is this supposed to be the night you can't go on?

## TRADITIONAL TRAINING AND SERVICE

*This is the working of Idolatry.*
*O my love*
*I am sorry I asked you*
*to live with me in the snow*
*and that I worshipped the snow*
*This is the working of Scorn*
*The Lord is faster than you*
*This is the working of Sloth*
*So swift these tears*
*So calm this grief*
*This is the working of Compassion*
*I will go behind the mask of your anger*
*I will go behind the mask of your revenge*
*I will dwell in your heart and your halfness*
*This is the working of Marriage*

## TRADITIONAL TRAINING AND SERVICE

*It is a bed of longing*
*I lie on every night*
*The Ghost of Absent Woman*
*squats upon my lap*

*With the weight of memory*
*she bears her haunches down*
*but has no comfort for the one*
*she heaves her fancy on*

*(Kingston, Ontario, 1973)*


*the memory of you*
*waiting for me on your stomach*
*the picture of our love*

*(Athens, 1975)*


*I studied my desire*
*one yellow afternoon*
*when I no longer wanted*
*you or anyone*

*Many people called me*
*or sent their shadows here*
*shadows well defined*
*voices very clear*

*The sun was in the curtain*
*with some shadow leaves*
*I touched myself un-*
*til your form appeared*

*(Los Angeles, 1975)*

155

*So it is you. You waiting for me. You small. You crouching. You looking up. You drawing the veil of womanhood around you as if you were coming out of the bathtub with a towel. I will have to go looking for you again. I'll have to lift you up and see where you are sitting. See what you're sitting on. Threads and seeds. It makes you grow. No, it's you. Speaking to your hand in the pool. It does your bidding. It creates a fountain. But the fountain won't go high as your throat. I miss you. I could have omitted your nipples. Now I want you. Why don't you welcome me. I know you did. Why don't you now. There's something wrong with your hand. It's working uselessly above the water. I will do its bidding. It is a gentle view of slavery. You can't be comfortable, can you. Now I taste you. You want to keep the men strong. That is the basis of your resistance. You have a good handshake. You want me to fight for you. Keep still. You won't keep still. Your ideas are crumbling. You are starting to believe what you think. I say no. Your appearance is flimsy. It won't do. Who told you you could build a tower with that one hand. That's one of those ideas that has made you unhappy. Hurry to me again. This time I want you to drink my seed. I've said this before to someone else, but I could travel with you. You must push your mouth out. It's all that is missing.*

*(Mt. Baldy, Calif., 1976)*

156

# NOW I COME BEFORE YOU

Now I come before you
I move into the gloom
My liberty my curfew
Both within the room

Sorrow with a compass
Anger with a sword
They lock me in a harness
They draw me to the Lord

Other angels tend me
Nausea and Fear
No one can defend me
From your judgement here
*
Your harness I despise
The angels you assume
What darkness you devise
For this your little room

Better sing a money tune
Or light a cigarette
Than raise a moon upon this ruin
That all the walls forget

Order in the family
Freedom in the spheres
Stretch your skin in front of me
For two and forty years

I am the voice you put away
Because it was too mad

But what I have or had to say
Is all you ever have or had
              *

Grave decision to be holy
Rebel cry to storm the sky
Boring tracks of reason's folly
Stumbling back to wonder why

Discipline and masturbation
Orgy and the distant cool
All that's in and out of fashion
Silver tongue or priestly drool

Come to me or leave me waiting
Pride upheld or pride dissolved
Stinking cretin or your captain
With the wind and waves involved

Only to be here approaching
Only to be where you were
Be your most unchosen orphan
Murdering his father, Sir
              *

Glory to your perfect prison
Glory to your perfect hell
Glory to the fierce decision
Underneath our lives and all

Mercy mercy on your creatures
Judge the world from every heart
Bless us with your gentler measures
Keep our lives and deaths apart

Humiliate our high belief
Humiliate our doubt
Oh give the treasure to the thief
And let the keeper out


## NOW I COME BEFORE YOU


*This was written in the light of her Purity, using some ruined conventions, which, in the leisure of her Love, he was able to restore*

It is all that connects them now
It is only here that the Marriage can be repaired
This is the working of Sunday School

which is so beautiful that you can't stop reading. I killed her. I fucked her. I told her what to wear, the white not the grey. A woman in the hated bed. Defeat. Goodnight.

Stepped out on the street just as J. was stepping out on the street a few houses up. She was beautiful again. She was alone and everyone was asleep who had claims on either of us. We hurried from each other lest we betray them. The bathroom mirror immediately. Yes, she saw you at your best, your scarf well wrapped.

If only he would give up this religion of his, if only we could get him back on amphetamine when he wrote like an angel

## WHICH IS SO BEAUTIFUL

*The betrayal was not always deferred, as we learn from*
*the yellow Secret Pages of July 1973:*

> what a lovely way/to earn a living/sitting in the
> sunny garden/thinking about your cunt
> the enemy is close/be careful of the net/I am still
> in servitude/My delightful pleasure with you/secret
> and stolen
> held by a wife/in the closet of language/looking out
> at the mysterious world/through the windows/of
> what we did last night

*No one ever saw this page before tonight. I just turned off*
*the radio. It has to be quiet so I can study what it means*
*not to be forgiven. O love, there was*

a flaming sword which turned everyway

*when I tried to explain the sorrow*

# THE REBELLION

It was a terrible rebellion
I rebelled against a sentence
    between her legs
I punished myself with a holiday
I took a ghost to bed
and caught the seed in the palm of my hand
Her green cotton dress was pulled up
She sat on my face all night long
She dragged me to Jerusalem
and married me over and over
while the silver star of Bethlehem
coughed and spat
in a smoker's reveille
and the priesthood forced me to resume
my old domestic conversation

## THE REBELLION

*It is interesting to see how he loosened these shining lines from a long dull confession in The Garden section of the original manuscript of My Life in Art. It is the summer of 1975:*

I rebelled against my situation. I rebelled against her skin. The nettles gave me a nasty sting on my way out here. A calm day, modest day, no sun, but no menace in the overcast. All the colours have surrendered, like one of Anthony's paintings. I rebelled against my sentence in the garden. I was on a hundred planes out of here. There is a snail on a leafy weed. The bumble-bee tries to loosen a bud's tight aperture. It tries twice. I cut my foot on something sharp on the beach of Monica's freckles.

Yesterday my dark companion told me to come quickly and quietly, but I missed what she tried to save for me: two sparrows mating in the eaves. "Have you ever seen them fuck?" She used her fingers to evoke the shuddering tail feathers. Her green cotton dress was pulled up. "I'm sunning my bum. I don't know why it's bumpy."

I rebelled against Domestic Conversation. All is calm now. I chained myself to the stone floor for an hour and a half. No butterflies, not that I care. Ants have emerged. I haven't seen them yawn. The sun comes through weakly. There's a butterfly, a small white one, too white. I am grumpy because I cannot indicate the vastness of my heart.

It was a terrible rebellion. I hated the daisies. I punished myself with a holiday. I took a ghost to bed

163

and caught the seed in the palm of my hand. It's suddenly noisy with the sweet strains of bird, wind, and radio. I tried to crush her into some confession I cannot even imagine, an unconditional apology for making a wound and making a nest in the wound. I forgot I was meant to marry her in Jerusalem. This is supposed to be the reward of the spirit. I am furious. I'll sell a million copies. The bumblebee, or one resembling it, has succeeded in prying open the bud. I thought I was speaking to you from a plateau of resignation but I notice that my eyes have become slits and I am gritting my teeth. This damn case fits right over me, this iron spirit maiden.

As the daisies grow higher an untidy aspect of the garden is revealed, things fallen, crushed, dried, tangled...

*He cleared the garden, perfumed his anger, established her sexual beauty, raised the graven image of a spiritual worker among the daisies, and began to worship it.*

# ACROSS THE STREET (1975)

I am across the street. Across the street from her. January in Montreal. Snow between us. Reach deeper into the building to. To what? Find me? The snow melted but it got cold again and it started snowing tonight. It's quiet. It's much more quiet than you think. Snow has covered the frozen grass on the square. Why don't you look at the square? Very formal. Very beautiful. Study of benches, metal fence, and trees against the lamplit snow. "Meditation on a Wintry City." Reach deeper into the building. Recover your straight back. The voice that has no quarrel. Why are you pretending to make a life without me? The solemn city landscape under the window. Very formal. You will be electrocuted if you try to touch a description. You like to think of me as the Virgin of a small altar. You can handle that. You kneel among the people. This is acceptable. The candles. The pressed trousers. Not acceptable. It hurts the head not to be truly among them. A debate whether or not the light should be closed and the desk turned toward the window. Resolved. Leave the room altogether. The kitchen is warmer. Stand beside the water heater waiting for me to speak. What vow could you keep? To fast? To do pushups? To listen for me like a goodbye? Whether or not you believe in miracles. Debate. So deep is your habit of leaving me. So shy to approach. So attached to your headache. What vow? To be faithful to her as she is faithful to you. You forgot the things you taught me. You forgot your noble birth. And now she begins to remind you. An unexpected source of dignity. This paragraph is not inconsistent with your alleged intention of singing songs to women. You may stand beside

the chieftain. They need to be told it is good music.
Don't quarrel outside. If only it was tomorrow. If only
the girl from La Jolla tapped on the windowpane. Not
the dreaded stream. The new music. The courtyard to
her Presence. You may stand up straight. There is a
second's worth of pride here. You may use your mind.
It is not forbidden, you know. Watch your mind care-
fully as once again you enter the room with the view of
snow and iron fences. It's not beautiful enough. It's
like me. It's your whore telling the story. Don't leave!
Don't summon your fatigue. It could be quiet here.
You could really rest. You could speak of objects. The
water heater. The stove. The smell of white paint. If it
wasn't for me you could leap to conclusions.

*ACROSS THE STREET*

You like to think of me as the Virgin of a small altar.

> I kneel in the great market
> The Virgin moves her mouth
> to give me courage
> I sacrifice a tiny disgrace:
> the final ruins of my song
>
> Take these relics from my hand
> You Who Give Birth To God
> The old chords, the used-up words
> Put them back again
> into the unmade world

*(New York, 1970)*

166

Sleepless, with appetite imperial
the woman in the moon could not confine
(although I wanted her to rise and fall
for me, she would be one more concubine)

I looked at all the stars on wires drawn
down the sky, around, and up again
and thought how faint their light compared to one
unborn, to her with whom I have not lain

*and these lines from the original manuscript of My Life in Art, written in the summer of 1975:*

D. was the usual Italian queen bee. I am tired of the Madonna. They all want a cathedral for their little brief miracle. They love to see a man walking toward them with a stone on his back and a candle in his hand...

*but such bitchiness dissolving into:*

Mary, mother of, in your blue, whenever you want me to think of you, you put sopranos and a French horn section into my lust. I look up. There you are, standing in your blue between a robe of frozen water and the black winter bark. I kneel down with the rusted stars, another ambition-crazed animal brought down gracefully to the forest floor, and whoever was the girl under my fingernails, she stands up in her blue frozen waterfall with a baby made of dust...

# THE PRICE OF THIS BOOK

I had high hopes for this book. I used to be thin, too. I thought I might live in one place and know one woman. I walked through the starlight this morning. I made my way through the lambs to the slanted concrete floor. I had on my red apron and I had the woman I loved. I wanted to end it, but it would not end: my life in art. I had pledged my deepest health to work this out. The working was way beyond this book. I see this now. I am ashamed to ask for your money. Not that you have not paid more for less. You have. You do. But I need it to keep my different lives apart. Otherwise I will be crushed when they join, and I will end my life in art, which a terror will not let me do.

## THE PRICE OF THIS BOOK

*In the early pages of the Final Revision of My*
*Life in Art, we have this variation:*

Speech of the Final Revisionist. I had high hopes for
this book. I used to be thin, too. I thought I might live
in one place and know one woman. I walked through
the starlight this morning. I made my way to the
Meditation Hall. I had on my black robes and I had
the woman I wanted. Another exquisite ordeal. I
wanted to end it, but it would not end, my life in art. I
had pledged my deepest health to work this out. The
working was way beyond this book. My heart had
sailed beyond these pages but the flight was too fragile
to carry a man...

*The price of this book is high, too high to be*
*useful, too high to be kind. The silence of thoughtlessness*
*and the voices of the Easter sheep — what, besides Mental*
*Pride, is served by such a substitution? This is the false*
*marriage of the Manifest and the Unmanifest.*
*Abominations are born from this union. This kind of*
*thought permits anything to appear, but it does not*
*require the thinker to appear with it. Uniforms appear,*
*and jackboots, but no one has to march and no one has to*
*look. Paragraphs that create the bonfire should also*
*create the piss*

# FORMAL IN HIS THOUGHT OF HER

I am certain he will never have her, this man
who sits before the window with his pen and ink,
who has been listening ever since the night began
to the crickets and his clock going in and out of sync.

Look how he is formal in his thought of her.
She makes her way through darkened embassies.
His stunning polaroids demagnetize and blur—
That could be anyone between her knees.

She does not overwhelm him with her absence.
She does not keep him raw as she did once.
He's raised a customs house at every entrance
to search and tax her beauty if she comes.

He is as tired of his longing as her absence
and so are we. Let's go get a drink
and leave him to his altars and his incense
and his crickets and his clocks going in and out of sync.

*Roshi poured me a glass of Courvoisier. We were in the cabin on Mt. Baldy, summer of 1977. We were listening to the crickets.*

    —*Kone, Roshi said, you should write cricket poem.*

    —*I've already written a cricket poem. It was in this cabin two years ago.*

    —*Oh.*

*Roshi fried some sliced pork in sunflower oil and boiled a three minute noodle soup. We finished one bottle of Courvoisier and opened another.*

    —*Yah, Kone, you should write cricket poem.*

    —*That is a very Japanese idea, Roshi.*

    —*So.*

*We listened to the crickets a while longer. Then we closed the light so we could open the door and get the breeze without the flies coming in.*

    —*Yah. Cricket.*

    —*Roshi, give me your idea of a cricket poem.*

    —*Ha ha. Okay:*

—      *dark night (said Roshi)*
              *cricket sound break out*
              *cricket girl friend listening*

    —*That's pretty good, Roshi.*

—      *dark night (Roshi began again)*
              *walking on the path*
              *suddenly break out cricket sound*
              *where is my lover?*

    —*I don't like that one.*

—          *cricket! cricket! (Roshi cried)*
*you are my lover*
*now I am walking path by alone*
*but I am not lonely with you*

*—I'm afraid not, Roshi. The first one was good.*
*Then the crickets stopped for a while and Roshi*
*poured the Courvoisier into our glasses. It was a peaceful*
*night.*
*—Yah, Kone, said Roshi very softly. You*
*should write more sad.*

# DAILY COMMERCE

The white truck from Interstate Meat Co. The wind and the sun in the leaves of the maple tree. A sparrow lands beside a shimmering green garbage bag. Bicycle conference at 4294. Truck from Total Transport. The milk from the broken bottle has dried in the street. Here it comes, the truck from Allen's. Here it comes, the truck from Iberville Lumber. Green delivery van from Abrams Kosher Meat. Sun ascending toward noon. Fast-moving blue van from Courvette Plumbing. Green van from Oriental Trading Co., this information taped to rear window. Simpsons' van. Superior Brush Manufacturing Co. St. Hyacinth Express. Clarke Traffic Services pulls away with boasts written upon its side. Blue taxi. Peepee in our alley by baby sponsored by male parent. Firetruck returns. Mysterious grey sealed van from ARCA. Benfeito Grocery in red. From the houses on one side to the houses on the other fly the sparrows. Fast-moving saffron-coloured VW. Chambly Clothing Co., a white truck. A red dump truck, E. Mercier in small yellow letters. Leonard Auto Supply, clean and yellow. Les Huitres Océanne Enrg, with a picture of a dish of them, against the sea-blue tin. Ford Station Wagon parking. M. Aucoin, green van. S. Rioux, plumbing and heating. Two sparrows on the wire that passes through the maple tree. Sun climbing high. Here it comes again, Interstate Meat Co., western beef choice red and blue, all written in black but red. Blue extermination van. F. Crepeau Transport is done, it roars away. The wind lifts up all the leaves toward the sky, and then forgets. JAWA Motorcycles, World's Champions, red and white. Big truck from Howicks, 7300 Hutchison, Montreal. O a heavenly Chinese girl with mother and infant passes below this balcony, black hair and I am nothing to her. Peepee child and father loitering in their own doorway. Top of pointillist poplar sighted above the roofs of west side of street, it accepts the crown from the invisible hands as sudden trumpet music from the radio calls up the martyrs, and the vague clouds kneel down. Some vans or trucks went by unnoticed. A loud Plymouth. Plombier Lecuyer. It's noon exactly. Noises from the birds, singing, enthusiastic. Something self-satisfied about the sun. Automatic Mailing and Printing Co., white and black van. Lasalle Taxi. Regal Taxi. Hardtop Cadillac, wine-coloured. Another fire truck returns. Blue Levine Bros. Bakery. Blue Imperial. A tire screech on Rachel Street. Fuck You painted on a Mach 1 fender in drippy yellow. Let the beautiful girl in the green Renault look for me. H. Laroche, carrying furniture. On its mission, a beige unmarked van. Rainbow General Transport, huge and blue, unloading. --ntiac, letters missing on the back of a yellow one, carrying a man and a woman. Jules D'Alcantrara, fleuriste, filled with cold flowers. Deluth Meat Grocery. Nea ZoH, that is, New Life Supermarket. Fatima and Vinga Food Products. Not to have those legs around me, or the flimsy tunic fall for me, or never to outwit her schemes for lives in houses such as these, and better and better. Matador Converters Co., Quilters, dark truck

## DAILY COMMERCE

*This is the land of work. This is where I*
*get down to it, where I am not ashamed*
*to speak of my balmy love, or to try*
*it out on all that my greed has inflamed.*

*So the Chinese girl is unmolested*
*and her life turns out okay without me,*
*my dark erection unmanifested*
*except within the pants of poesy.*

*Glory to the maple tree on my street*
*filled with wind, sun and the sparrow birds.*
*Glory to daily commerce and the fleet*
*of trucks, the chiefest subject of my words.*

*This is the land of work. I sit apart*
*from you and long for you with all my heart.*

# THIS WRETCH

In love with the women of other men. Once it was an affliction. I hated my envious heart. I love you J. I love you D. How brave they are, the custodians of your beauty, the men whose diaries I no longer read. I am in debt and self-disgrace. I do not want my wife or baby. How sweet to be this wretch, sitting at midnight in an empty house, forgotten by himself in the midst of his own testament.


## THIS WRETCH

*I'm fucking the dead people now*
*not you with your breast on fire*
*not you with your blouse on the floor*

*Why do you ring the bell in the night*
*as if we lived in a town*
*as if the Infant were born*
*as if the Mystery survived*

*I'm fucking the dead people now*
*I don't have to try for a song*
*I don't have to count up to ten*

*Why did you let your fingers grow*
*Why do you wear your jeans so round*
*There's snow on your eye. Your underwear*
*is cold especially the rim*

*Not waiting for a parachute*
*Don't want to scrape off the moon*
*Try to die on your stomach*
*I'm fucking the dead people now*

176

## EARLY THIS MORNING

Early this morning I sat in the basement.
I gave the woman honour.
I affirmed she was the one.
Instantly the pardon came.
Married in the invisible world,
                    my work was plain.
My wife slept.
My son clapped his hands over the jam.
I practised in the highest court
                    with pick and harmony.

## I'M GLAD I'M DRUNK

I'm glad I'm drunk
I need to be drunk
to tell you that I'm finished
to tell you that I'm through
but I'm not drunk enough
to tell you about the snake
wrapped around my asshole
and I'm not drunk enough
to tell you that it's okay
it's okay it's okay darling

I can't drink what I have to drink
to be drunk enough
to curse the hummingbird
and the whole fucking Creation
emanating from its iridescence

I'm going to tell you
even if I fall on my face
that I invented sky writing
I did it because I fell in love with you
and I'm not afraid of losing you

# I'M GLAD I'M DRUNK

*This is preceded by the following entry in the Brentwood Journal of 1977:*

I took 140 mg. of caffeine and 75 mg. of Phenyl-propanolamine at 9 a.m. My meditation was painless except for the dull thud of horror in my heart. I'm in the driveway again. I'm speeding away. I'm breaking my neck on the chain.

I want to finish the songs. I want to be in a song. I want to be singing my heart away. I want to ---- my wife all the time. Will she desire me ever again? In the old dark way? In the old blind way?

The Irish are speaking to me again. The ones who are always in tune. The ones who are terribly drunk. The ones who aren't even fun.

It isn't enough to ---- your wife. It isn't enough to speed along. There isn't enough in the Irish tongue. The trees will never be green enough. That's why I can't complain. Love is all overlooking. That's why I can't complain.

Hurry to your dinner. Hurry to your food. Finish the feeble prayer, your stonework, your golem duties to the woman being born. Hurry to the thigh in the plate and the cloudy city. Lean over your round world. Cut off rusty talk with the unfucked woman, the unconvinced friend, the countless uncertain universes, avoid diplomacy with them. Hurry to your appetite. Hurry to your birthright and the night of long knives and grease. Hurry, worker in the realms of song. Hurry angel, covered spirit, minstrel of my greasy pilgrimage. And hurry back to the warm bed where she is sleeping, where it is dark, her face turned away, and you meet in half sleep, kind to each other as if newly met. Sleep against her back, your arm across her waist, your hand under her breast. Until she thrashes in her sleep. The flies walk over your face. She does not know how to make you comfortable. She never has. Hurry to sleep. Find a way to get upstairs. The bells have rung, the faithful are breathing frankincense. In a crack of the wood shutters the morning has begun. Hurry to your stretched-out nakedness and to lightly touch yourself as will some time the woman being born. Jiggle your knees, mind worker, hurry through your testament. Invent your song. Invent your power. Hurry to be born in the bed beside her. Hurry to the fish hook. Hurry to your destiny. Hurry to your cunt. Hurry to your vision of God. Time is like an arrow. Hurry to the bank. Hurry to your unborn children. Hurry to your thin body and your suntan. Then the slugs will dance, the pure night sky will not mock you. Hurry to your discipline and your bland regime. Move faster than the stain, the fat, the disappointed heart. Hurry to the peanut butter and the cool summer drink. Hurry to your miracle. Hurry to the empty stomach, the victory fast, the unbuilt temple. Wake her up and quarrel in your bed. Eat together through the dark. Seize the round world and stop it from struggling and plant your mouth in the burnt skin. I am your dead voice.

## HURRY TO YOUR DINNER

*Many thanks for deserting the tongue. Many thanks for the calm breathing of the defeated intelligence. Many thanks for clear intellection in the realms of loss. Many thanks for keeping still while a flood carried off the world. Many thanks for restoring every detail of what it was before.*

# SLOWLY I MARRIED HER

Slowly I married her
Slowly and bitterly married her love
Married her body
    in boredom and joy
Slowly I came to her
Slow and resentfully came to her bed
Came to her table
in hunger and habit
    came to be fed
Slowly I married her
sanctioned by none
with nobody's blessings
in nobody's name
    amid general warnings
    amid general scorn
Came to her fragrance
    my nostrils wide
Came to her greed
    with seed for a child
Years in the coming
and years in retreat
    Slowly I married her
Slowly I kneeled
And now we are wounded
    so deep and so well
that no one can hurt us
except Death itself
    And all through Death's dream
I move with her lips
The dream is a night
    but eternal the kiss
And slowly I come to her
    slowly we shed
the clothes of our doubting
    and slowly we wed

## SLOWLY I MARRIED HER

*It's a long way home down Fairfax to the Santa Monica Freeway, a sinister stretch of the Imagination. The twine of her fragrance sparks above me like an old streetcar cable. Dust of L.A. exhausted springtime in the lever of my headlights, lifting her shade from smoke to smoke among the luminous lane markers. And what is this song but a little night Muzak for those who get out too much, who talk to their divorced wives disembodied between the windshield and the following stars in voices of secret intimacy such as they never used in the everlasting regime of parting*

# THE TRANSMISSION

The transmission is weakest in those passages where the reader is swept along in the story and the insights and the flow of events. We know what is best for the type of person who will put his arm into this pile of shit. His greed must be blocked at every turn. He must remember who he was before he started taking drugs and listening to the slogans. He must take a good deep breath before he walks away. It is his own shit, preserved forever like the body of Lenin in the centre of downtown. Above all, we must not let him anaesthetize himself with the luxurious notion that he has been in the presence of unruly genius.

# THE TRANSMISSION

received from Nadab and Abihu as they cried
with one voice out of the consuming fire of punishment

received from the king of Ai as he hung from a
tree fully embraced by the reality of his huge mistake

received again and again from the circles of
Noah's raven

received from the riot of women in Samson's
heart

received from the high forehead of David's
giant

and still the heart does not open

received twice from Amnon and Tamar, one
pressed on the other, once in the form of loathing, once in
the form of desire

received from Solomon in the strategy of his old
age: the worship of women

received from the first veiled bride whom the
bridegroom did not love

received directly from the honeycomb

received without a language in the Vehicle of
Ignorance

and still the heart does not open

received on the crown of my head from the lips
of an eleven-year-old woman in the dark pine fragrance
thirty years ago

received through the crystal of my child's first
snowstorm

received from the one who destroyed The Letter
of Consolation, saying: There is no consolation, there is
no need of it

and still the heart does not open

received from the music in my mother's wrist

received from Rosengarten's measuring stick which is unmarked like the fretboard of a cello

received from Hershorn as he covers his head and begins to live without a wife

received from the buttocks of my dark companion as she dances with my head in the presence of other men

and still the heart does not open

received and received

until we come to the heart that does not need to open

received in six tongues of smoke from the cedar guitar of the dancer's fiancée

received from the eternal smoke of violins and shoes and uniforms

received from the extra light of Jesus Christ failing into the extra world of pain in the new formation: Be your enemy

received from the consecrated ground of a buried pig

received and received

until we come to the heart that is free from opening

## THE TRANSMISSION

*I was arrested for kissing a broom.*
*The judge said, "Were you the bride or the groom?"*
*I thought for a while and I finally spoke:*
*"Judge, I don't have to listen to that kind of joke."*

## THE PRO (1973)

Lost my voice in New York City
never heard it again after sixty-seven
Now I talk like you
Now I sing like you
Cigarette and coffee to make me sick
Couple of families to make me think
Going to see my lawyer
Going to read my mail
Lost my voice in New York City
Guess you always knew

## THE PRO

*from the Nashville Notebooks of 1969:*

I leave my silence to a co-operative of poets
who have already bruised their mouths against it.

I leave my homesick charm to the scavengers of
spare change who work the old artistic corners.

I leave the shadow of my manly groin to those who
write for pay.

I leave to several jealous men a second-rate legend
of my life.

To those few high school girls
who preferred my work to Dylan's
I leave my stone ear
and my disposable Franciscan ambitions

# THE MOUTH OF THE CAVE

Rachel and Raymond in Montreal cruising the socialist meetings. Krantz and Ingrid in Way's Mills, both under the spell of her prowlike breasts. Anthony and Christina watching sunsets over the cold wine. Yvette and Tiler on a pile of stolen wives. Irving and Aviva in Toronto amazed at the duration of the siege. The heart with its pendulum of genitals. Steve and Jacqui saying, That's what we need. Malka and Kid in New York to re-negotiate, waiting for the baby. My love in a dark bikini. My love with the banner of Justice. Margerie and Brian, the wife and the sailor, the old arrangement of voyage and waiting. Hartman and Francine, her victory, his divorced shade, the house on Westmount Avenue. Cork and Sheila on the East Side, Jimmy Baldwin coming for dinner. Lucy and Peter, she fucked all the sailors on the honeymoon cargo. Adam and Eve standing in prayer at the mouth of the cave all night long. I will thrill you. I will ignore you. I will forgive you. The children come forward. You are my father. This is my body. This is my understanding. They make love under the windmill at the age of ten. Sam and Sonia going back to Rome. Sophia and Michel choose a black governess. Margaret and Gerald, vegetarians, decide on an abortion. Willie Fork talking about the smell of her cancer, the receptacle strapped to her leg. Dick and Joy, and who is the real poet. The sunset begins. The waves work less and less. The colours of the wall and the colours of the tablecloth jump forward. The girls leap on and ride them tightly. They commandeer the event. The fall into darkness is the setting for their eternal discipline and victory. We grab our small cold glasses and try hard to be hypnotized.

## THE MOUTH OF THE CAVE

*variation:*

> The heart with its garland of genitals. The clock
> with its testicle pendulum.

*deletion:*

> Let us meet the women
> Men are dead and we prefer
> the other kind of human

189

# MY LIFE IN ART

This is the end of my life in art. At last I have found the woman I was looking for. It is summer. It is the summer I waited for. We are living in a suite on the fifth floor of the Château Marmont in Hollywood. She is as beautiful as Lili Marlene. She is as beautiful as Lady Hamilton. Except for the fear of losing her I have no complaint. I have not been denied the full measure of beauty. Nights and mornings we kiss each other. The feathery palms rise through the smog. The curtains stir. The traffic moves on Sunset over painted arrows, words and lines. It is best not even to whisper about this perfection. This is the end of my life in art. I am drinking a Red Needle, a drink I invented in Needles, California, tequila and cranberry, lemon and ice. The full measure. I have not been denied the full measure. It happened as I approached my forty-first birthday. Beauty and Love were granted me in the form of a woman. She wears silver bracelets, one on each wrist. I am happy with my luck. Even if she goes away I will say to myself, I have not been denied the full measure of beauty. I said that to myself in Holston, Arizona, in a bar across the street from our motel, when I thought she would be leaving the next morning. This is drunken talk. This is Red Needles talking. It is too smooth. I am frightened. I don't know why. Yesterday I was so frightened that I could hardly hand a Red Needle to a monk on Mt. Baldy. I'm frightened and tired. I am an old man with a silver ornament. These stiff movements should not be accompanied by tiny silver bells. She must be plotting against me in my bed. She wants me to be Carlo Ponti. The black maid is stealing my credit cards. I should go sailing alone through the pine trees. I should get a grip on myself. O god her skin is soft and brown. I would sell my family graves. I am old enough for that. I am old enough to be ruined. I better have another drink. If I could write a song for her I could pay for this suite. She saw the men in Afghanistan, she saw the riders, how can she stay here with me? It is true I am a hero of the Sahara but she did not see me under sand and fire, mastering the sphincters of my cowardice. And she could not know how beautiful these words are. Nobody could. She could not perceive the poignant immortality of my life in art. Nobody can. My vision of the traffic on Sunset Boulevard through the concrete lilies of the balcony railing. The table, the climate, the perfect physique for a forty-year-old artist, famous, happy, frightened. Six in the morning. Six-o-five. The minutes go by. Six-ten. Women. Women and children. The light gone from Los Angeles they say, the original movie light, but this view of Sunset Boulevard satisfactory in every way. My life in art closing down. Monica sleeping. All the wandering mind is hers. My devotions begin to embarrass me. She should grow tired of them soon. I am tired of them now. She is pregnant. Our love-making is sweet because of this. She will not have the child. Six-twenty. We drink Red Needles every night. She tells me of the gay San Francisco world. The weight of her beauty has become intolerable. People in the liquor store actually pop-eyed and double-took as she went by with her long hair and her sacrificial child, her second-hand clothes and her ordinary face mocking all the preparations for allurement here in the heart of Hollywood, so ripe she is in the forces of beauty and music as to frighten me, who has witnessed the end of his life in art. Six-forty. I want to go back to bed and get inside her. That's the only time there's anything approaching peace. And when she sits on my face. When she lowers herself onto my mouth. This feels like doom. This is a pyramid on my chest. I want to change blood with her. I want her slavery. I want her promise. I want her death. I want the thrown acid to disencumber me. I want to stop staring. Six-fifty. Ruined in Los Angeles. I should start smoking again. I'm going to start smoking again. I want to die in her arms and leave her. You need to smoke a pack a day to be that kind of man. When we were on the road I was always ready to drive her to the nearest airport and say goodbye but now I want her to die without me. I started my exercises again today. I need some muscle now. I need a man in the mirror to whisper courage when I shave and to tell me once again about the noble ones who conquered all of this.

*I saw Roshi early this morning. His room was warm and fragrant. Soon he was hanging from a branch by his teeth. That made me laugh. But I didn't want to laugh. Then he was playing my guitar. From above he looked old and tired. From below he looked fresh and strong. Destroy particular self and absolute appears. He spoke to me gently. I waited for the rebuke. It didn't come. I waited because there is a rebuke in every other voice but his. He rang his bell. I bowed and left.*

*I visited him again after several disagreeable hours in the mirror. He hung from the branch again. He looked down fearfully. He was afraid of falling. He was afraid of dying. He was depending on the branch and on his teeth. This is the particular self. This is the particular trance. He played my guitar. He copied my own fingering. He invented someone to interrupt him. He demonstrated the particular trance being broken by the question: What is the source of this world? He asked me to answer. His voice was calm and serious. I was so hungry for his seriousness after the moronic frivolity and despair of hours in the mirror. I could not answer. Difficult, he said, reaching for his bell. I bowed and left.*

# THE NIGHT I JOINED

The janitor was saying how much he loved the king the night I joined the Party. Down in the basement the Commissar forced an old comrade to drink urine the night I joined the Party. A wave advanced on Pakistan and a master of the highest state advised that nothing changes the night I joined the Party. The dove came down on the workers' café and I crossed myself with a woman's hand the night I joined the Party. My wife spoke to the lawyer and my daughter had no underpanties on under the clothes of her first communion dress the night I joined the Party. I myself was calm, I wasn't angry anymore, I was tired, I took up my pen, my sacred pen, my pen of intricate love, my pen of longing, and that was the night I joined the Party. Those concerned mainly with beauty forgot who I was, I myself forgot who I was, I even forgot the star-ringed nipples of the girl I didn't get, and they scratched my name off the bronze memorial to the fallen sparrow the night I joined the Party. Because I could not stand the boredom of the right and the boredom of the night I joined the Party. The little ghosts of crickets sang Another Man Done Gone, and pebbles flew from my forehead against the stained-glass windows of the C.I.A. on the night that I joined the Communist Party.

194

# EVERYTHING THAT IS UNENGAGED

Everything that is unengaged
comes to the service
of one
    who makes no claim
The pimps of revolution
& the scabs
    of capital gain
they struggle with
what was used up long ago
but the petals of
tomorrow morning's morning glory
illuminate the corners
    of my useless days
My wife returns
    on the boat of our mistakes
We meet beneath
    the Bridge of Sighs
The age returns
when we did make
    a unity of various desires
The age returns
    with dark-red cherries
of the New York summer
with oils and powders
    of an intimacy
that would not decline
even through the gravities
of distance hate & jealousy

    *and look, dear heart, how the virgin*
*she takes him into her gown*
    *and see how the stranger's armour*
*dissolves like a star falling down*

Nuit Magique, Montreal, 1978

# HOW TO SPEAK POETRY

Take the word butterfly. To use this word it is not necessary to make the voice weigh less than an ounce or equip it with small dusty wings. It is not necessary to invent a sunny day or a field of daffodils. It is not necessary to be in love, or to be in love with butterflies. The word butterfly is not a real butterfly. There is the word and there is the butterfly. If you confuse these two items people have the right to laugh at you. Do not make so much of the word. Are you trying to suggest that you love butterflies more perfectly than anyone else, or really understand their nature? The word butterfly is merely data. It is not an opportunity for you to hover, soar, befriend flowers, symbolize beauty and frailty, or in any way impersonate a butterfly. Do not act out words. Never act out words. Never try to leave the floor when you talk about flying. Never close your eyes and jerk your head to one side when you talk about death. Do not fix your burning eyes on me when you speak about love. If you want to impress me when you speak about love put your hand in your pocket or under your dress and play with yourself. If ambition and the hunger for applause have driven you to speak about love you should learn how to do it without disgracing yourself or the material.

What is the expression which the age demands? The age demands no expression whatever. We have seen photographs of bereaved Asian mothers. We are not interested in the agony of your fumbled organs. There is nothing you can show on your face that can match the horror of this time. Do not even try. You will only hold yourself up to the scorn of those who have felt things deeply. We have seen newsreels of humans in the extremities of pain and dislocation. Everyone knows you are eating well and are even being paid to stand up there. You are playing to people who have experienced a catastrophe. This should make you very quiet. Speak the words, convey the data, step aside. Everyone knows you are in pain. You cannot tell the audience everything you know about love in every line of love you speak. Step aside and they will know what you know because they know it already. You have nothing to teach them. You are not more beautiful than they are. You are not wiser. Do not shout at them. Do not force a dry entry. That is bad sex. If you show the lines of your genitals, then deliver what you promise. And remember that people do not really want an acrobat in bed. What is our need? To be close to the natural man, to be close to the natural woman. Do not pretend that you are a beloved singer with a vast loyal audience which has followed the ups and downs of your life to this very moment. The bombs, flame-throwers, and all the shit have destroyed more than just the trees and villages. They have also destroyed the stage. Did you think that your profession would escape the general destruction? There is no more stage. There are no more footlights. You are among the people. Then be modest. Speak the words, convey the data, step aside. Be by yourself. Be in your own room. Do not put yourself on.

This is an interior landscape. It is inside. It is private. Respect the privacy of the material. These pieces were written in silence. The courage of the play is to speak them. The discipline of the play is not to violate them. Let the audience feel your love of privacy even though there is no privacy. Be good whores. The poem is not a slogan. It cannot advertise you. It cannot promote your reputation for sensitivity. You are not a stud. You are not a killer lady. All this junk about the gangsters of love. You are students of discipline. Do not act out the words. The words die when you act them out, they wither, and we are left with nothing but your ambition.

Speak the words with the exact precision with which you would check out a laundry list. Do not become emotional about the lace blouse. Do not get a hard-on when you say panties. Do not get all shivery just because of the towel. The sheets should not provoke a dreamy expression about the eyes. There is no need to weep into the handkerchief. The socks are not there to remind you of strange and distant voyages. It is just your laundry. It is just your clothes. Don't peep through them. Just wear them.

The poem is nothing but information. It is the Constitution of the inner country. If you declaim it and blow it up with noble intentions then you are no better than the politicians whom you despise. You are just someone waving a flag and making the cheapest appeal to a kind of emotional patriotism. Think of the words as science, not as art. They are a report. You are speaking before a meeting of the Explorers' Club or the National Geographic Society. These people know all the risks of mountain climbing. They honour you by taking this for granted. If you rub their faces in it that is an insult to their hospitality. Tell them about the height of the mountain, the equipment you used, be specific about the surfaces and the time it took to scale it. Do not work the audience for gasps and sighs. If you are worthy of gasps and sighs it will not be from your appreciation of the event, but from theirs. It will be in the statistics and not the trembling of the voice or the cutting of the air with your hands. It will be in the data and the quiet organization of your presence.

Avoid the flourish. Do not be afraid to be weak. Do not be ashamed to be tired. You look good when you're tired. You look like you could go on forever. Now come into my arms. You are the image of my beauty.

## HOW TO SPEAK POETRY

*I did not want to appear again in these pages except to say goodbye. I thought that he should be left alone in this most delicate phase of the wedding preparation, with the man asleep and the woman being born. I thought he could be trusted to maintain the balance. He can't. It is too quiet for him. He has to shoot off his fucking Sunday School mouth. We're supposed to sit back and listen to The Good Guy talking, the old crapulous Dogma of Decency. This filth cannot go unpunished. How dare he summon the widows of Asia to his side! How dare he break his vow of silence to lecture, in the name of The People, from the shit-stained marble balcony of his obscene cultural delusions! I hate him for this. He will pay for this religious advertisement. He will carry the syrup of it in his balls. He will pass this life as a teddy bear. Death to the Commissars of the Left and the Right! Death to the Commissars of Mystery! I hate his fucking face, all serious with concern. Don't let him into the good movie, and don't let him hear any of the merry tunes in the Music Hall. Never let him sing again. And let him sit outside with his stinking educational corpse while the stripper on the little gilded stage turns every one of us on.*

# THE ONE IN THE YELLOW SWEATER

Three young village girls come to my window again. This is the third time. They squeeze together and look down into this stone room. Two of them flee. The one in the yellow sweater locks her eyes into mine. She insists. Perhaps she is nine years old. We look at each other for long seconds. She wants to exchange the seed gaze, deliver to each other our longing to be born in truth. Her companions return to tear her away. My head clears. The birds sing deliriously. The calm blue sky seals the top of the exterior wall neatly with nothing to be desired. If she comes to look at me again maybe I will have the courage to greet her as she greeted me.

I saw her again the other afternoon. I was balancing my son on a wall of the terrace so he could see the cats and chickens in the yard across the way, and there she was in the street below, peeking in the window of my basement room to see if I was there. We saw each other from the wrong angle and there was nothing for either of us. She ran away. Her narrow hips intrigued me, but only my grosser appetites, those devoted to God and Beauty.

I have locked myself in here for a week. It is a foul sunken pit. It is now the sixth day of a cosmetic fast. My face is too fat. Foul sunken pit is not a metaphor for solitude. The room is below street level and I have just fouled my trousers for some odd nervous reason.

She just came to the window! the blonde child with four or five friends. I could hardly see their faces, the light was all in here and none on the street. I couldn't tell which face was hers, was somewhat relieved—I knew I couldn't summon a greeting. Then she tapped on the window, I saw which one was her, and she called my name—Leonarde, good health to you! and they ran off.

# THE POLITICS OF THIS BOOK

Years ago I sat in this garden, at this very table, among the ancestors of yellow daisies that surround me now. I was drugged and happy then. I wrote deep from my sunstroke. Enough of the past. It is a morning in March 1975.

The bumblebees have arrived. There are noisy birds in the rain gutter. One thread of a spider web, suddenly white, goes fishing in the sunshine. Some butterflies want to fertilize my shiny boot. A cat sharpens the top of a wall by walking across it, and then by walking back adjusts the horizontal.

I won't be sitting here long. I'm in a terrible hurry. I'm going to Jerusalem. I'm going with the happy Israeli soldiers and I'm going with the King of Saudi Arabia to kneel down in the place that we were promised.

A bee enters a hanging yellow flower like a woman pulling a gown over her head, shivering, struggling upwards. The sun climbs to the middle of the sky and stops. It's noon. It's the first bell of noon ringing loud from the cathedral tower. The second. The third. Great shovelfuls of sound dumped into the grave of our activity. The sound fills up every space and every thought. The seventh. The eighth. The future is blocked. The past is plugged up. Layer after layer of the present seizes us, buries us in one vast amber paperweight. Sealed under twelve skyfuls of the only moment.

I won't be going to Jerusalem after all. You will have to go to Jerusalem alone. It is yours. It was given to you by the angels of culture and time. But I can't go. And I can't loosen your interest in the war. You will want to see corpses, the oldest tourist attraction, and you will want to "challenge the sphincters of your cowardice under sand and fire." Goodbye.

I will be here if you look back, at this very table, in this very garden where the bumblebee charges like a bull into the yellow trumpet, and the sun makes a dent in my black trousers, and my wife repeats on a loop, "Did you smell the ambrosia of the universe in my little cunt?" and the birds tune up at last.

# ALL SUMMER LONG

All summer long she touched me
gathering in my soul
from many a thorn and thicket
with fingers quick and cool

The light came from her body
the night went through her grace
All summer long she touched me
I knew her face to face

Her dress was blue and crystal
Her words were few and small
She is the vessel of the world
and mistress of us all

All summer long she touched me
The flame was on her heart
She graced me with her company
When all men stood apart

# IF I AM NOT HER SERVANT

You do not visit me
The kingdom is overturned
The woman is dead
Her palace burned

Her breasts are nailed
to a bulletin board
In her cunt
a cigar is stored

I can't believe
I stare and mumble
Beauty in such disarray
Love so humble

O rise up from
the general massacre
Resume her radiant form
and be her

From whispering hearts
gather her cancelled graces
from our corpulence
her crystal spaces

Anxious desire
let her light caress
and music revive
in the creases of her dress

May I serve her
both sides of the grave
If I am not her servant
I will be another's slave

Glory and glory to her
who gives birth to god
who bends down over
the world's huge wound

My love my love
initiate her reign
Come back to me
Come back to me again

## IF I AM NOT HER SERVANT

the difference between you and a vampire
your mouth open and black
    vampire sleeps sometimes satisfied
but you never do
on your dark lips
all the sweetness of the dreaming boy
    the dreaming girl

your mouth is a bowl of blood
and all your poor ones pressed against the window
sickened with eternal hunger

like a lipstick print on kleenex
like a bad experience with fishhooks
is the way I remember you

I got away from you
the way these lines get away from you
by grace and sweat and hatred

your cunt is not my home
it never will be

*:from An Angry Conversation with Lilith, 1973. Lilith
enjoyed this talk immensely. Our poet tried so hard to be
polite. Actually all that he wanted to do was touch her
spirit through the portal of the rose, emblem of surrender
in some peoples' books. Finally she turned her back on
him and he experienced her compassion. As for me,
personally, I am pleased that you have all had the
appropriate adventures with each other's bodies. I hope
that you will continue to be able to lose your selves in the
anatomy lesson. Goodbye and goodbye and goodbye.*

# THE CENTRES

The centres of the daisies have begun to fall apart. Behind a layer of cloud the sun looks like a full moon. Between two mauve poppies you receive me into your world. I sink into my fur collar. Please do not mix a girl's name into the fragrance of the morning. Some-one slams a carpet. A loud bee works among the yellow bugles.

My dark companion presents me with a plate containing a stunned and hideous centipede, "scissors" as they call them here, the ugliest creatures that I know. I would like not to want to kill it, but I want to, so I do. I slip it onto the ground and I pound it with a rock. Now what will happen to me? I am knighted. I am given a glimpse of my true appetite. Lines of light break through a fault in the clouds. I am shoved into the world with the duty of keeping my mouth shut.

Now there is a pleasant commotion of music and town bells, roosters and a new volume of sunlight. A shepherd's song on the neighbour's machine. You let me rest in sight of your throne. In sight of a blueprint of your throne. You attack me for boasting. You throw out my shoulder as I bend my head in prayer. I witness the destruction of a full-blown mauve poppy. The wind breaks the hinges of the petals and they fall. My dark companion signals me from the terrace, a lamb across her shoulders, standing in a hail of marble dust.

*Worship me here*, says the Lord two years later. *My world is one.*

## ONE OF THESE DAYS

One of these days we're going to get outside. We'll take off your shoes and listen to the wind chimes in the garden. The dust of vanished jet planes will be a glaze around the street lamps. The little star of Karl Marx will light a corner of the vault. We'll lie beside the shed mingling our conversation with the soft round noise of the neighbour's doves. Adam's father will be feeling better. So will Adam's mother. Our rugged life in the back yard is about to begin. We're going to dig a lily pond if we can get outside. You can see us in our chairs now, immensely attractive and paralysed. There we are reflected in the windows of the room. We'd weep over the story you could tell about us. You'd be so pleased to meet people who do not wish to govern you.

# YOU'RE NOT SUPPOSED TO BE HERE

You're not supposed to be here
Not supposed to be looking for me
This is the poor side of silence
This is the white noise
            of the abandoned appliance
This is The Captivity

You need details
You need the name of a street
You're not supposed to be here
            in the Name of God

You're waiting for me again
Waiting at the mouth
            of the Tunnel of Love
But where is the cold little river
Where is the painted boat

If only the hummingbird
would sip at your desire
If only the green leaves
could use your longing
If only a woman were looking
over your shoulder
at a map of the Eternal City

It seems that nothing can take you away
from this odd memorial
Nothing that's been made or born
separate you from
            the fiction of my absence

All the Messiahs are with me in this
You're not supposed to be here
All the Messiahs agree
You're not supposed to be looking for me

# FINAL EXAMINATION

I am almost 90
Everyone I know has died off
except Leonard
He can still be seen
hobbling with his love

*I have examined his death. Although it is
unstable, I doubt that we shall find the old goat nibbling
again at the lacy hem of the various salvations. I am more
vulgar than he was, but I never pretended to a spiritual
exercise. Furthermore, his death is sexless and cannot be
used in politics. There is a cheap sweet smell in the air for
which he bears some responsibility. I swear to the police
that I have appeared, and do appear, as one of his voices.
I see in the insignificance of these pages a shadow of the
coming modesty. His death belongs to the future. I am
well read. I am well served. I am satisfied and I give in.
Long live the marriage of men and women. Long live the
one heart.*